SOME OF MY BEST FRIENDS ARE GOTHS

(30 ESSAYS IN 30 DAYS)

by TIM BRIFFA

Voltone Books

All rights reserved. No reproduction, copy or transmission of this publication may be made without written permission. No paragraph of this publication may be reproduced, copied or transmitted save with written permission or in accordance with the provision of the Copyright Act 1956 (as amended). Any person who does any unauthorised act in relation to this publication may be liable to criminal prosecution and civil claims for damages.

This book is sold subject to the condition that it shall not by way of trade or otherwise, be lent, re-sold, hired out, or otherwise circulated without the publisher's prior consent in any form of binding or cover other than that in which it is published and without a similar condition including this condition being imposed on the subsequent purchaser.

Copyright @ Tim Briffa 2006

Contact timbriffa@hotmail.com.

Made and printed in Great Britain.

CONTENTS

INTRODUCTION 4
1. SIMPLE ANSWERS TO COMPLICATED QUESTIONS 6
2. THE CRIKEY MAN 10
3. AGONY UNCLES AND FLEETWOOD MAC'S GREATEST HITS 13
4. THE STORY OF GI 18
5. HAMSTER GASSING 24
6. COMING TO LONDON 28
7. HOW THE MUSIC INDUSTRY DESTROYED ROCK 'N' ROLL 37
8. CHRISTINA AT THE BUS STOP 46
9. HOW TO EAT A LIGHT BULB 49
10. AIMS, AMES AND AMIE 55
11. DIRTY NEEDLES AND THE HATCHAM SOCIAL CLUB 59
12. HOW TO PICK UP GIRLS Pt. 2 62
13. BUSKERS WILL BE PROSECUTED 80
14. WHO WRITES THE SONGS? 83
15. THE TEACHERS WHO TAUGHT ME WEREN'T COOL 91
16. IF YOU WANT TO GET ON, GET A HAT 99
17. MY LIFE WITH THE BEATLES 105
18. CHELSEA, SQUATTING AND A VERY BAD DAY 126
19. THE FIVE CATEGORIES OF RELATIONSHIP 138
20. DOWNSIDE 143
21. KELLY 153
22. A VERY MAD WEEK 156
23. PREDICTING MUSIC FASHIONS 162
24. MADNESS ATTRACTS MADNESS 168
25. WEIRD SHIT HAPPENS 179

26. CHEYLESMORE	189
27. BEACON	192
28. POLL TAX RIOTS	197
29. MY DRUG HELL - THE EARLY YEARS	207
30. DIGGING FOR SQUIRRELS	219
POSTSCRIPT	237
END NOTES	237

INTRODUCTION

My name is Tim Briffa. I sing and play guitar for a band called My Drug Hell. A few years ago a song of ours 'Girl at the Bus Stop' made Number 1 Most Requested on a handful of US radio stations and was also used in a Miller beer ad and a couple of films. There was other good stuff happening in the UK and Australia, and for a while it was all looking very promising, but then we had a run of bad luck culminating in our UK label going bust just before the album was released and the band breaking up.

I put together a new line-up, but it never quite gelled, and we now have a new one and seem close to finishing our long overdue second album.

I documented the period around the first album and an extremely fucked up relationship I was going through in a set of diaries I've since named *My 'My Drug Hell' Hell*. They need editing, though, and I've never tried to get them published. I've also written a couple of (unproduced) film and TV scripts, and I'm part of the way through an ambitious book on where science, religion and philosophy meet.

As a way to get something finished and out there, I recently wrote a play - *How to Pick Up Girls* - which I figured would be fairly quick to write and easier to get produced than a film or TV series. Things worked out, and it had a two-week run in a theatre in Camden. It was great seeing people laugh when I wanted them to laugh or shocked when I wanted them to be shocked - an artist needs an audience or there's no point.

But I'm starting to feel like I could use another boost, and as the science and religion book is driving me a bit mad and I'm also waiting for a tape machine to be repaired so can't record at the moment, I've come up with an idea for a new writing project inspired by a book of essays I just finished called *I Love You More Than You Know* by Jonathan Ames.

So I don't spend too long on it, I'm setting myself the task of writing one essay a day for the next thirty days, beginning tomorrow. Even if it turns out rubbish, at least a month from now I'll have a finished book to my name and my CV won't look quite so slim.

Tim Briffa, 26 Sep 2006

SIMPLE ANSWERS TO COMPLICATED QUESTIONS

Wed 27 Sep 2006

I'm semi-seeing a half Sri-Lankan girl I met recently at a '70s club called Heavy Load. Unlike the arts type crowd that mainly go there, Michelle works in finance and has a degree in science, which I actually like as it means we can have conversations other than the usual "so what bands/films are you into at the moment?"

The other morning we got into an interesting one about the evolution of camouflage before getting on to more familiar ground (for me certainly) - the difference between men and women, in particular regarding sex. I was saying men are more into one-night stands than women, while she said women enjoyed them just as much - "We're just better at hiding it."

I've heard other girls make this kind of claim. To support it, they'll sometimes mention some supposedly "wild" friend of theirs they'll insist is "just like a man" sexually because they once slept with their plumber or something and have had as many or more one-night stands than most guys they know. The fact they describe them as "like a man" shows it's less common for women to behave like this - more's the pity. What they also overlook is how much easier it is for a woman to get laid than a guy - precisely because men are so much more into casual sex and rarely turn down a decent offer.

So, for example, if she's had fifty one-night stands, that's probably about as many as she's wanted to have. But if a guy's had fifty, he'll have had to try it on with at least ten times that number, and even that will just be a tiny fraction of the women he'd like to have slept with but didn't bother approaching because he knew they'd have just told him to fuck off.

I realise not every guy feels like this. In fact, Michelle then told me about some male friend she said never sleeps around, even when he's had the opportunity, and finds the whole idea of casual sex "empty and depressing." I know guys like this, but, again, they're the exception, and in most cases I suspect it's more to do with how difficult/impossibe they find it to get laid on any regular basis. Rather than deal with the frustration of being constantly rejected, they start to switch off that instinct altogether and resign themselves to a life of monogamy as their best chance of guaranteeing regular sex. But put them on a tour bus with Kiss with hot babes coming up each night going, "So what are you doing after the show?" and it would be a very different story.

To be fair, Michelle actually is quite "male" in her sexuality and can at least talk from experience. I still couldn't convince her she wasn't typical, though. We continued batting the argument back and forth, when I remembered something she'd told me the previous night about her flatmate coming in drunk one time and offering her ten quid for a blow job. So I asked if she'd ever heard of a woman offering to pay a man for oral sex. She admitted she never had, which seemed to finally settle the matter.

She went to make some coffee, and when she came back said there was a question I could maybe help her with. "Why is it that a guy can go for years trying to shag everything that moves and freaks out if you even mention the word 'relationship', and then, all of a sudden, they announce they want to settle down, and the next person they go out with, they get engaged to — even if they're not nearly as nice or pretty as the one before?" She was clearly speaking from personal experience, so I asked if any of them had just turned thirty or hit some other landmark age.

"Yes, as a matter of fact. One just turned thirty, and the other's about a year older. How did you know that?"

I suggested they'd reached some age which they'd expected to have settled down by, or else they'd seen some other sign of their mortality and impending physical decline — their first grey hair or a slightly receding hairline and then thought, "It's all downhill from here, better hang on to the next one before my options dry up completely."

Michelle didn't seem too cheered by my theory. "Do you really think it could be that simple?"

"Possibly," I said, and suggested someone conduct a study to see if there was a link between men settling down and the initial onset of hairloss. "They could call it 'Baldness: The number one cause of marriage'."

I was being flippant, but it wouldn't surprise me if there was a correlation. People often expect some deep explanation to these kinds of questions, but I reckon there's often a much more mundane one, especially when it's something like losing your hair, which can affect people profoundly, but isn't something most guys would feel comfortable discussing.

There was some French philosopher who after hearing about someone who shot himself after farting at a dinner party, developed a theory that rather than the big existential questions, "Is there a God?" etc., what caused the most unhappiness in the world were embarrassing physical conditions they couldn't talk about openly.

It makes sense to me, especially when you think about what's out there. Along with flatulence, there's incontinence, constipation, piles, fissures, jock itch, yeast infections, STDs, sexual dysfunction and for women various menstrual-related issues - all extremely distressing potentially, and none of which can be mentioned in polite company.

I left Michelle's around the early evening. She invited me to stay, but I said I had some work to do. It was Sunday, and I could tell she didn't believe me. She probably thought it was something she'd said or that I was going off her, but the real reason was much simpler: I really needed a shit, and felt embarrassed doing it at hers.

THE CRIKEY MAN

Thurs 28 Sep 2006

About two weeks ago, the Australian wildlife presenter Steve Irwin died after being stung in the heart by a manta ray. He'd built his reputation on the fearless, some felt foolhardy, manner in which he'd prod and poke various deadly Outback creatures - spiders, snakes, crocodiles, etc - in order to reveal just how dangerous they can be. When inevitably they'd snap or lunge back at him, he'd somehow always manage to dodge out of the way. Despite having apparently come within inches of his life, he'd then give some comically understated response: "Whoah! This feller seems a little upset," perhaps, or a simple, "Crikey!" - becoming something of a catchphrase.

In spite of the tragedy of his passing, it was hard therefore to miss the irony that of all the creatures you might expect to have caused it, it proved to be something as innocuous as a ray, lending the story a David-and-Goliath-victory-for-the-common-fish-type twist.

I came in last night and happened to catch the end of an interview with Steve's wife, now-widow, her first since his death, apparently. It was one of those "I'm Barbara Wintergreen from CBN" pieces with that yellow-green cast for some reason you only get with US news reports. There was something else I found odd, because while both the interviewer and Mrs Irwin referred several times to the shock and devastation she was currently experiencing, I could see few outward signs of it. There were no bravely fought-back tears or a slight cracking in her voice at each mention of his name, nor did she look especially grim-faced for someone whose husband had died barely a fortnight ago. If anything, I'd say she was looking rather good on it, or "chipper," to use an Australian term.

The more I thought about all of this - plus the fact that the interview must have taken a few days to arrange, meaning she'd have been discussing appearance fees, exclusivity rights, etc. even closer to his death - the odder it all seemed, such that it was the first thing I mentioned when I spoke to my dad earlier today. It turned out he'd caught some of the interview on another show in which she'd apparently said something about just wanting to "move on with her life and be happy." Now, I realise grief affects people differently, and far be it for me to say how she should be dealing with hers, but if I was Steve looking down, I don't think I'd be too pleased with all of this. It's not that I'd be expecting her to spend her entire life mourning my loss, but having given the best part of mine loving and taking care of this person, I think I'd like a fair amount - more than two weeks' worth, certainly - before she started talking about just wanting to "move on with her life and be happy."

But I really shouldn't judge because who knows what really goes on in another person's relationship. If the way he treated those animals was any indication of his sensitivity, she may have every right not to be feeling too cut up right now. More likely, it just hasn't sunk in yet. But if there is any truth to what I'm saying, she wouldn't be the first person to find herself in such a situation. For some reason it's assumed if someone's partner dies unexpectedly that they had this wonderful, idyllic relationship, but you only have to study the divorce statistics to know this can't always be the case. I'm not saying they'd be happy if their partner died suddenly, just not as devastated as most imagine.

And there's some for whom it really would be cause for celebration - those in love with someone else or caught in some bitter empty-shell marriage they daren't leave because of the legal or financial repercussions. For them, the sudden death of their partner must feel like being handed the most amazing get-out-of-jail-free card. Not only do they get to keep the money, house, assets and full access to the kids, they may also be in line for a big, fat insurance cheque to begin their new life with that mistress or toy-boy lover they've had to keep secret all these years.

But instead of cracking open the bubbly and hitting the town, they have to wear this grim facade and feign devastation every time someone asks them how they're coping, which can't be easy to maintain. There must come a point when they ask themselves how long before it's acceptable to be seen having a good time without everyone thinking they're some cold-hearted monster. There are cultures where spouses have to wear black or go around wailing for a set grieving period. It doesn't seem so strange, thinking of it in these terms.

AGONY UNCLES AND FLEETWOOD MAC'S GREATEST HITS

Fri 29 Sep 2006

A couple of days ago I had a call from an "ex" called Kim inviting me to her birthday party this weekend. She also said she had some news regarding her new boyfriend. "You won't believe this. Jorn just said he loved me! And I didn't have to cry or squeeze it out of him or anything!" - a personal reference that made me laugh. She also said he'd brought up the subject of having children, something she's always wanted, and said that for the first time ever that she felt "on the same page as a guy at the same time."

It was nice to hear her sounding so happy as we had a few ups and downs when we were together, and argued quite a bit. Initially this centred on my continuing to see other girls. She was no angel herself in this area, it has to be said, and had a particularly annoying habit of fucking various "friends" of mine - though when she did it, it would still somehow end up being my fault.

We eventually agreed to stay exclusive, which calmed things down for a while, but the rows soon started again, this time mainly about the fact we'd never been on holiday together. I like to go on holiday alone, it's one of the few times I get to fully clear my head. But as the main thing I was trying to clear my head from was the arguing, this created something of a Catch-22.

She then said she could accept us not going on holiday if I let her move in with me. I was not keen due to a previous bad experience, but I eventually agreed. Of course, instead of stopping the arguments, it just gave us a whole new load of stuff to disagree on. When we weren't rowing, we actually got on really well. The sex would be good, and we could talk for hours. The rest of the time, the sex would be crap and we'd just get on each other's nerves. I used to think of it as two cogs that weren't fully aligned. We'd engage for a while, and then we'd separate and start spinning away at our own speeds. This made it very hard knowing what to do. Just when I'd be thinking, *All we do is argue, might as well end it*, the cogs would re-engage and we'd be back to having a great time.

This went on for a couple of years when something happened that finally convinced me she was not 'the One' and we could never make things work. I'd just returned from playing a couple of gigs in Paris to a noticeably cool reception. There was also nothing in the fridge - not even some milk to make myself some coffee. I went out to get some and when I came back, she was dancing away to *Fleetwood Mac's Greatest Hits* which she had turned up to near full volume. Had it been one of their earlier albums with Peter Green or even *Rumours*, I might have handled it. But at that moment nothing seemed to illustrate better that we were close, but not quite close enough, than hearing that particular album blasting from my stereo.

I told her straight: it was over. We'd had some trial break-ups before this, but for the first time she didn't try to dissuade me. She just said "okay" and quietly began packing her stuff. The next day I discovered why she'd taken it so well, when I happened to see her in a club, dirty dancing with some guy she'd met while I was in Paris.

There was a period of mutual mudslinging after that, but we got through it, and I now count her as one of my best friends. I even helped her get together with Jorn.

She'd called one time to say she'd met this really cool photographer at a party in the block where they both live. She ended up in his flat where she said they had the best sex of her life (a detail I could have done without). There was only one problem: he already had a girlfriend, who he continued seeing despite being, in Kim's words, "really boring and not all that."

She wanted to know why he'd choose the not-all-that girl over her (Kim has done modelling work and is definitely hot). He'd also barely even acknowledged her on the few times they'd since crossed paths. I said there were a few possible reasons, but couldn't really say without knowing more. She became more and more obsessed and began thinking they were destined to be together, which isn't as strange as it sounds. As well as living in the same building, there'd been a few odd coincidences. When she'd asked to see his work, a couple of photos were ones she'd cut out of magazines as a teenager and stuck on her bedroom wall. At the same time, she knew she might just be blowing the whole thing up in her head.

Then one day she called saying there was another party coming up which she'd been told he was going to and that his girlfriend would also be away that weekend.

"This could be my only chance," she said. "I need a way to get his attention and make him like me!"

She'd said she'd asked a couple of her female friends what to do, and both said to make him jealous by playing hard to get. I groaned and said that women always recommend this as the best way to get a guy, because it's what works for them. When they see a man acting distant and aloof, they assume he has some mysterious, magical quality. But when we see it, we just assume the girl is up her own arse or doesn't like us, and if anything, it puts us off.

She then said she was thinking of trying to impress him by mentioning the business she runs (she recently set up a designer bag company).

"Men don't care what a woman does for a living."

"Really? What if I just tell him straight - I'm in love?"

"Do not do that."

"But I'd love it if a guy said that to me. So what should I do?"

I told her that men think mainly with their dicks, and if they're happy on a sexual level, they start to become more involved emotionally (sometimes). As she had such a narrow window of opportunity, I said she should give him the most direct no-strings-attached sexual offer she could and suggested sending him a text near the end of the night saying, "Come to mine. I really need to fuck you."

"But what if he's not into that? Not everyone's a filthy pervert like you."

Kim can also be quite pervy, so I asked if she'd really want to be with someone who didn't respond to an offer like that.

"Probably not."

"Then if it doesn't work, you'll know he wasn't meant for you."

"Yeah, I suppose."

In the end she toned it down to something like "Come to mine. I need to be with you," but it worked, and they ended up having more amazing sex. Soon after, he ditched his girlfriend, and now he's declaring his love and talking about having kids together.

Believe it or not, Kim's not the only girl who asks me for relationship advice. One even asked if I'd act as an Agony Uncle for a radio show she's trying to set up. If I'm any use, it's probably because I remind them not to project - as Kim and her friends were doing.

Guys do this too, which is why you'll sometimes hear them going on about some girl they're convinced is "completely gagging for it" and are then surprise when they make some lewd comment and she walks off in disgust.

My philosophy is very simple: we are like mirrors of one another. What sex is for a guy, love and romance is for a woman. Men prioritise sex. We want it as early as possible and start to become more emotionally involved if we're satisfied on that level.

Women prioritise emotions. They are quicker to become emotionally attached, and if they're fulfilled on that level, get more into the sexual side.

If the woman isn't satisfied emotionally, she'll start to look around even if the sex is good, while the man will lose interest if he's not fully enjoying the sex, no matter how much love she gives him. (Things change as we get older, and our relative testosterone and oestrogen levels change, but that's another story.)

The simplest way to get someone interested is to offer what they want - a blowjob or casual sex for a man being roughly equivalent to flowers or a romantic dinner for a girl (and vice versa), and hence my suggestion to Kim.

The principle also applies to jealousy. Nothing pisses a guy off more than the thought of his girlfriend having sex with a random stranger, while her main paranoia is usually the guy having some kind of romantic encounter or "developing feelings" for someone.

Neither sex is morally superior. Men are often dismissed as more shallow because it's usually us trawling bars looking for easy sex, but women can be every bit as desperate and conniving when trying to secure something long term.

Obviously, I'm generalising a lot, and we can all behave like our opposite from time to time, especially if there's a strong attraction. The yin/yang symbol is another way of looking at it - with the white spot in the black area representing the bit of feminine contained in the male and the white spot representing the masculine within the female. If you fall in love, you start to form a more balanced whole and there is less need for compromise as you tend to want the same thing. If you're lucky, you end up "on the same page at the same time."

To be honest, I'm not sure if that's how the symbol is meant to be interpreted, but it's the way I view it, and as a basic rule of thumb, I find it very helpful.

THE STORY OF GI

Sat 30 Sep 2006

About five years ago I was incredibly fortunate and inherited my uncle's house, and I just received an email from a former tenant called Gi.

At the time she was working as a lap dancer in the West End. I've known a few girls from that industry and seem to have a sixth sense for spotting them. I've often picked them out in cafes, bars and even on the tube - which might not sound hard, but when they're not working, they're often dressed down in some unflattering baggy top or tracksuit and little or no make-up, presumably because they get so sick of being hit on at work, the last thing they want is to encourage it when trying to unwind. But like the smell of smoke when you've been in a club, there's this aura of sex that seems to cling to them which my filth antenna homes in on.

That's basically how it was when I first saw Gi. I'd just arrived at a warehouse party organised by some friends in Kings Cross when I saw her on the opposite end of the room dancing away in an oversized puffa jacket and a cap pulled over her eyes. Although I could barely see her face, I couldn't stop looking.

Ordinarily, I'd probably have gone over there to check her out, but I'd come with a French girl, Judith, who'd been staying at mine the previous week. We weren't "together" as such. In fact, she had a boyfriend in Paris who she was due to return to the following day. However, we'd had a fling in the past which we'd revived the first night she stayed. Although we'd continued sharing a bed, it had definitely run its course by this point, at least as far as I was concerned.

I should also mention that it was her who asked to stay at mine - and originally for just two nights. For some reason the place she was meant to go on to fell through, and rather than throw her onto the streets, I said she could stay until she'd found somewhere else. She seemed to take this to mean "stay as long as you want" because from what I'd seen, she hadn't so much as rung a hotel to enquire about rates.

I'd hoped at least to be free for this party, and while technically I was - given our history and that this was now her last night - I was fairly sure she wouldn't have been happy if I spent it chasing some dirtball in a puffa jacket.

I then saw Dave, our bassist, who Judith knew from Paris. We all chatted, and then I went to get some drinks. As I was waiting to be served, Gi appeared next to me and introduced herself, though as "Victoria" (her "working" name).

We immediately got into a deep conversation about art and film, though it felt like there was a sexual undercurrent, and my filth radar continued bleeping away - such that I ended up asking her outright if she worked in porn. She denied it, though. After about ten minutes I said I should rejoin my friends but would look for her later so we could continue the conversation. About an hour later some friends of Judith appeared, so I went to find her again.

We'd been talking for a while when we were joined by a raven-haired friend of hers (who was also scoring high on my radar). She asked if they could have a private chat. A couple of minutes later Gi came back. "Listen, my friend wants to leave, but you can come with me. We can get a hotel room or go to yours; it's up to you."

There's not many things I find as erotic as a straight-up offer of no-strings-attached sex ("filth on a plate" as Dave and I call it). I've had girls say stuff like, "Do you want to come back to mine and listen to some music," and though you know sex is likely, they can always change their minds. "What do you mean you thought we'd be going to bed? I only asked if you wanted to hear some music!" It's hard to claim a misunderstanding when hotel rooms get mentioned, so it killed to have to turn it down.

I explained the situation with Judith, how we weren't really together, but we'd had a fling in the past, and it was her last night, etc. I asked if we could meet another night, any night pretty much, and the sooner, the better. It wouldn't be as erotic as leaving there and then, but it could still be good.

She seemed cool with it and asked for my number. I wrote it down (I didn't have a mobile then). I then asked for hers.

"You don't need mine. I'll call you," she said, a little more firmly than seemed necessary.

"But just to be safe, you might lose it or something."

"I won't lose it."

"You never know though. It would be a real shame if…"

"I won't lose it," she repeated.

Her attitude seemed to be toughening by the minute. The raven-haired girl who'd been listening to the whole conversation asked if she could have another word. When she came back, she'd hardened some more.

"I've decided I'm not giving you my number and I'm also not going to call you. Either you leave with me now or you never see me again."

"What? Why are being like this? You know I'd love to leave with you now."

"Then do it."

"But I told you the situation. I don't want to upset this girl."

"Then you never see me again."

"Now or never," interjected the raven-haired girl, who I was now starting to seriously go off.

"What's this got to do with you anyway?" I said.

"I'm looking after my friend. You should be grateful she's even considering you."

"Oh, for fuck's sake!"

They had another consultation, after which things went even further downhill.

"Okay. I'm going to give you fifteen minutes to make up your mind. If you don't come with me, I'm leaving with that guy over there" - she pointed to someone on the dance floor - "and that's the last time you'll ever see me."

"If you want to leave with him, that's your choice. I just don't get why you're being so nasty. Why can't we just meet another night?"

"Fifteen minutes," she said, and then the two of them headed towards the guy on the dance floor.

I couldn't work out how something so amazing had turned to shit so fast, but I had to make a decision, so I went to look for Dave. I figured he'd at least be sympathetic, but it wasn't to be.

"You can't do it," he said. "Judith will be gutted."

"But it's not like we're going out. She has her boyfriend."

"It doesn't matter. You know she's into you."

"But then I'll never see this woman again."

"Mate, she'll be fucking gutted."

The problem was that it was true. Whether or not she had the right, I knew she would be gutted if I left with Gi, which was why I hadn't already done so. For some reason I just hate knowing I've hurt a girl. I've stayed in relationships far longer than I should, just because I couldn't handle their reaction when I try to end it. The moment I see that wounded look in their eye and their chin start bunching up, I start to buckle.

It's cowardice, really - and also arrogance. Because when they say they'll never find anyone like me ever again, I think, *she's probably right,* and I feel like I'm ruining their life forever.

Of course when it does finally end, it's usually no time before they've found someone else and sounding far happier than they ever did with me, and I'm left wondering what happened to their declarations of undying love and why I didn't just leave when I felt like it. I've had this happen a few times, and this was not long after breaking up with Kim when it happened again.

As I was trying to decide what to do, this all came into my head, and it hit me that it was probably time I broke the pattern of putting other people's pain over mine. Sure, Judith would be gutted if I left with Gi, but then I'd be gutted if I didn't. And just because my pain was to do with sex, didn't make it any less.

I went to look for Judith, told her I was really sorry, but I was leaving with someone else and then walked away before her chin began to wrinkle. Which might not sound very heroic, but for me, it kind of was.

We got a cab to take us to a cheap hotel (dropping off the bitchy friend on the way) and then had a wonderful night of dirty porno sex.

The next day Gi was as nice as when we first spoke, and we ended up seeing each other for a while - in which time I learned her real name and what she did for a living. When that ended, she asked if she could rent a room and ended up staying for a couple of years.

She apologised numerous times for how she'd acted the first night. Though it was never directed at me, I did see the hard side reappear from time to time, nearly always after she'd come in from the club. It got so I could tell which nights she'd been working. When she realised this, it had a profound effect as she'd noticed other girls get that way after working in the industry for a while and swore she'd never let it happen to her. So she quit - much to her credit I thought, as it meant a big drop in earnings and stuff like having to buy her clothes from charity shops, which she'd never done before. It also meant she could no longer afford the rent she'd been paying me. Feeling partly responsible, I agreed to lower it.

Incidentally, after I left Judith, it turned out she forgot her keys and had to spend the night at Dave's (most of which she spent crying, apparently - he must have really been cursing me). The next time I saw her she was fine with me, though, and that night was never mentioned again.

In her email Gi asked if her old room was free to rent again. I said it was and because she is back to studying, she could have it at the old rent. I could probably have asked for more, but she's so much fun to have around I don't really mind.

HAMSTER GASSING

Sun 1 Oct 2006

I went to Kim's party last night. It was okay, but there weren't a lot of people and I ended up leaving around 1am. I wasn't ready to go home, so I called Michelle who was just leaving Heavy Load (the club where we met) and also looking for something to do. I suggested we meet at Oxford Circus and then look for somewhere in the area to get a drink.

It's hard to believe they've just relaxed the licensing laws. After wandering around Soho for half an hour, the best place we could find open was some goth/metal night at the St Moritz which we still had to pay to get into. I had a good time in the end, but I was getting heavy looks early on from some guy I once had an altercation with when he tried to get me thrown out of another club when I'd become a little rowdy (long story, won't bore you). In front of everyone I'd shouted, "Shut the fuck up, you're a Goth, you don't even count!"

I thought it was a good line, but when I told the story to Michelle, she suddenly looked hurt and said she used to be one. "That's okay," I said. "Some of my best friends are goths," which I also thought was funny, but it met an even stonier reaction.

While looking for a bar earlier, I found a pendant on the road in the shape of an owl. At some point I pulled it out, and Michelle said she'd had a pet owl as a kid, but her mum is from Sri Lanka where they're thought to attract evil spirits, and one day she came home to find her mum had given it away.

That led to a conversation about pet-related traumas.

We'd mostly had hamsters when I grew up, which as anyone who's kept them usually discovers are able to gnaw their way out of just about anything given sufficient time. Consequently, we'd regularly all be checking under cookers and behind fridges hoping to find Zog, Shredne Vashtar or whichever had done its Houdini act before it died of cold or starvation.

I was doing a search before school one day when I noticed something furry floating in a bucket of soapy water that my mum had left out the previous night.

"Mummy, what's that?"

"Nothing. A cloth."

At some point my neighbours bought one which they named Hammy (a little unimaginatively, I remember thinking at the time). Despite getting an expensive cage, he managed to escape and somehow then got through the adjoining wall, up a whole floor and onto my eldest brother's bed, who was asleep at the time. Luckily, he guessed it was Hammy and had the presence of mind to catch him. Not wanting to wake up the neighbours, he went to a little storeroom on the stairs and put him in a metal toolbox to deal with in the morning.

Being nocturnal, Hammy was soon clattering around inside and made enough noise to wake up my mum, who then woke my dad, telling him she thought there was an intruder. He picked up a metal bar he keeps for such a situation and was bemused to find Hammy had apparently locked himself inside a metal toolbox. Needless to say, it was all sorted out in the morning.

As they get older, hamsters can look pretty miserable as they start losing their fur, and their eyes sometimes bulge out. This is when most people take them to the vets to be "put to sleep." But my dad is an anaesthetist and couldn't see the point in paying someone else to administer the same drugs he used every day.

So it became an occasional family ritual that we would all gather round the dinner table where he'd have an old shoebox and some cotton wool which he'd then soak in chloroform. He'd place the wool in the box, followed by our ailing pet, and then close the lid while we stood around solemnly waiting for the shuffling sounds to stop.

I remember him removing the lid early one time. Like a boxer that had just received a knock-out punch, the little thing was standing, but motionless, and then keeled onto its side.

Michelle was a bit freaked out at the idea of my Dad euthanizing our pets, but I said it wasn't as strange as a story I once heard from a Dutch promoter called Ben.

We'd been staying at his flat, when Joe, our drummer, asked about a particularly mangey-looking stuffed stork that was out on his balcony.

"Ah, that! I keep meaning to bring him inside. He was my pet."

"You had a stork for a pet?"

"That's right. He used to follow me to school."

"Your pet stork followed you to school?"

"Yes, I raised him from an egg."

Every answer was weirder than the last, and then begged another question.

"You raised him from an egg?"

"Yes. When they hatch, the first thing they see they think is their mother, and then they follow them wherever they go."

"I've heard of that. I thought it was a myth."

"No, it's true."

I thought it might be a wind-up, but I know a bit about the subject, and when I pressed him, he had a detailed knowledge of both birds and the whole incubation process. But then the conversation took an even weirder turn. When I asked how the stork ended up being stuffed, he said his parents had done it, both of whom were amateur taxidermists, and they'd stuffed all his pets, having started with a hamster (funnily enough) and then moving on to various cats and dogs which they had placed around the house as ornaments.

It sounded like something out of *Tales Of The Unexpected*. After he left, we started talking about what it would be like growing up surrounded by all your dead pets and imagined Ben as a small boy, terrified of falling asleep lest he ended up alongside them - stuffed by his own parents.

COMING TO LONDON

Mon 2 Oct 2006

I mentioned before that I inherited my uncle's place a few years back. I don't feel deserving, but I can appreciate it at least as I've had quite a few housing issues in the past - especially when I first moved to London.

I came here a bit before turning eighteen with the intention of either forming or joining a band. I'd been planning this almost since first picking up the guitar and was so desperate to get started I was on the train to Victoria a couple of hours after my first dole cheque came through. I'd been offered three weeks of couch space at my sister's in Lambeth and another week at one of my brother's in Shepherd's Bush - but after that I was on my own.

In theory, I could have returned to my parents' in Crowborough, Sussex if things didn't work out, but that wasn't even a consideration in my mind. Because for as long as I'd been dreaming of getting into music, I'd been told that's all I was doing – dreaming. In varying degrees of subtlety I was accused of deluding myself by teachers, careers advisers, even fellow pupils.

A couple of months earlier a girl in my year had asked why I wasn't applying to any colleges. When I told her my plans, she said, "Ooh, expecting to find streets paved with gold, are you?" I was well aware of the slim odds of "making it," but that wasn't what was I looking for (or at least not the only thing).

These people caused me to doubt myself and over time their defeatist "you can't afford to follow your heart in the real world" attitude came to represent everything I thought was wrong with the world and was determined to avoid. Having railed against it for so long, the thought of returning home after just a few weeks, tail between my legs, would have been about as big of a humiliation as I could have imagined and a symbolic victory for their worldview.

So I wouldn't be tempted, I made a personal vow that I would sleep rough before coming back to ask for assistance. Whether I could have handled the reality of the cold, hard streets, had it come to that, I can't say, but I was dumb and proud enough back then. I think I'd have given it a try at the very least.

I tell you all this because it shows where my head was at the time and why I put up with what followed.

Aside from my brother and sister, the only person I knew in London was a guy called Paul who'd been to Downside, the boarding school I'd dropped out of two years earlier in favour of my local comprehensive. I rang to say I was in town and a couple of days later went to see him at his mum's place in Holland Park where we ended up getting stoned with a friend of his called Ramsay.

My own supply was getting low, so I asked if they knew anywhere I could score. Ramsay offered to drive me to the nearby All Saints Road, at the time a notorious police no-go zone where Rastafarians dealt from big bags of grass they'd carry around openly. He parked at one end, then told me to wind down the window. A couple of Rastas came over, and I negotiated a small deal. I went to take a note from my wallet, thinking I was being careful, but then an arm reached in and snatched it. I ran out after the guy, but he lost me in a side street.

I was literally down to a few coins, not even enough to get back to Lambeth, so Ramsay gave me a lift. The next day I jumped the tube with my guitar and made a pound or two busking which kept me going a couple of days when I found a lunchtime pub job that luckily didn't ask to prove my age.

A few days later I went to see Paul again. With him was another ex-Downsider called Nick. I never liked the guy, finding him pretentious and a snob, but he seemed pleased to see me for some reason, and when I mentioned I was looking for somewhere to live, he suddenly chimed, "Me too! We should look together. It's a lot cheaper if you share."

I wasn't exactly thrilled at the thought of sharing a confined space with someone I'd spent most of three years trying to avoid, but I knew I couldn't afford to live alone, especially since losing my wallet, and figured *better the devil you know*.

We discussed budgets. Nick had recently received a term's grant to study business in Egham, but due to expensive tastes and a growing fruit machine habit (the "fruities" as he called them), he'd blown almost half of it before the course had begun. We decided on a maximum total of £50 p.w. (This was the 1980s, so roughly double that for today's equivalent.)

Nick offered to buy *Loot* and the *Evening Standard* while I promised to check as many newsagent window ads as I could.

With just four days of grace left at my brother's, I was getting worried. So far we'd found just one place within our budget whose owner told us they had fifty more people coming to view that day alone.

As I was making my daily round of newsagents, I spotted a freshly posted ad:

```
Double room available opposite
     QPR football ground.
   £30 per week inc. bills.
    No gays or straights.
```

I was a bit concerned by the blatant homophobia, but the price was definitely right. The "no straights" part also appealed - a landlord who didn't just tolerate drug use, but actively insisted on it. How cool was that?

I arranged a viewing, and the next day we were greeted by a wirey Glaswegian with a greying ponytail.

"I'm Fran," he said. "Friends call me Franny."

Despite his slight frame and outward friendliness, he managed to exude a surprisingly strong air of menace. He showed us the front room of what was meant to be a one-bedroom flat, which was as depressing as you'd expect for that kind of money. It was obviously an illegal sub-let, as when I asked if I could claim housing benefit, he said, "No." I'd quit my pub job after leaving Lambeth, so until I found another, this meant I'd have just £9 left from my £24 p.w. dole money once I'd paid my share.

But the worst part was that the menacing, homophobic landlord came with the place, occupying an even dingier room at the back. All my instincts screamed "run," but we were out of options. Nick gave me a nod and I said we'd take it.

We never did get to Franny.

He was nice to us initially, though, popping his head in periodically to see how we were settling in, even passing on the occasional joint. But around three weeks in, the atmosphere suddenly changed when, without apology or warning, he announced the rent had gone up by five pounds. I now had just £6.50 a week to live on.

A couple of weeks after that, Nick came in to find the kitchen table had gone. He asked Fran what happened to it.

"Sold it," he replied matter-of-factly and walked off.

I'd been surviving on almost nothing apart from 17p packs of noodles or baked potatoes with margarine, so a kitchen table wasn't going to make a big difference to my life. Nick was very pissed off, though, as he wanted the table to do his course work on. (Despite the fact he'd only been into college twice since enrolling, he was still telling himself he'd be knuckling down at some point.)

I'd been going to the job centre every day, but work was getting very scarce at this time, so I was actually pleased when taken on as a fry chef at the McDonald's in Hammersmith for £1.55 p.h. before tax (no minimum wage back then).

I spent six days sweating away in a bri-nylon uniform and suffering various indignities, including handing out Ronald McDonald Happy Hats at a children's party, when they asked me to get my hair cut and I decided enough was enough. I'd found another part-time bar job that day at the nearby Lyric Theatre, so I knew I was safe. They treated me well, but the pay was about the same as McDonald's, and the shifts weren't guaranteed. Some weeks I made less than when signing on, so reluctantly, I went back to that.

I then discovered some of the joys of the UK benefits system. Because I'd left the job, I was declared 'voluntarily unemployed' and denied any money for eight weeks. I eventually won it back on appeal, but for a while my only income was from occasional busking forays that rarely yielded more than a fiver and which I had to keep to a minimum as I'd already received a caution.

If anything, Nick's finances were in an even worse state than mine. Having failed to curb his fruit machine habit, he was now surviving on handouts from a grandmother in Portsmouth who he'd visit every few weeks with the sole intention of tapping out a fifty. If she wasn't forthcoming, he'd actually ask to borrow money from me and would then piss me off further by sneaking out to the Princess Victoria down the road and shoving it into a one-armed bandit.

That wasn't his only bad habit. He'd constantly leave his dirty laundry strewn around the room (I once found a pair of his filthy socks on my pillow), then about once a month when he finally got around to picking it all up, he'd start having a go at me for not doing any cleaning. He'd also lapse into the pretentious smoothie act that annoyed me so much at school, going on about how much he loved the night - "I don't know what it is; I just love it!" - or some ludicrous statement about identifying with lions.

At the same time he could be a lot of fun - a valuable commodity when you can barely afford to leave the house. We started to develop a gallows humour about our pitiful existence - the two-bar fire we relied on both to keep warm and to dry our washing (ensuring almost everything we owned was covered in scorch marks) and the potato/noodle/margarine diet which Nick had now joined me on, and in a strange, Odd Couple-ish way, we started to get on.

We'd talk a lot about Downside, which I hated and he'd loved (naturally). He was curious about a streak I'd done through the main dining room (my final "fuck you" to the place) and then asked if I remembered our Headmaster announcing one assembly that someone had pushed an old oak teacher's table from a third floor window, reducing it to matchwood. I'd committed a fair few acts of wanton vandalism myself, but even I was shocked by this and wondered who would do such a thing. It was Nick, of course, plus another guy from our year. He explained that stuff they'd done had been mentioned in the previous two assemblies, so they decided to go for the hat-trick.

"What can we do that will guarantee a mention in this week's assembly?"

"How about we push a nice antique table out of a third floor window?"

Meanwhile, relations with our landlord continued to deteriorate. We'd usually check before entering any communal areas, but we'd run into him occasionally, and he'd either ignore us or snarl some words of abuse. Sometimes he'd be uncharacteristically nice, which we soon learned meant he wanted something from us and would then be followed by a request for some rent money in advance or to "borrow" some potatoes.

He'd usually add we should feel free to help ourselves to any of his food. This became a running joke between me and Nick, because there was almost nothing in his cupboard except for a pot of mustard powder, and his side of the fridge was also almost always empty, except every couple of weeks when a slab of red meat would appear - which he told me he would steal from a local butcher's while cycling past on his bike.

One time the bathroom light stopped working. We changed the bulb, but it still wouldn't work, so we figured it was probably something like a loose wire. We kept waiting for Fran to fix it (like us, he was having to light a candle every time he took a piss or had a bath). It was at least a month before he knocked on our door to announce he'd finally fixed it. The next time Nick went in there, he came back in hysterics. Instead of being constantly off, Fran had somehow wired it so it was now constantly on.

Nick could be very generous when he did have money. One time he returned from a successful Portsmouth visit with a big load of groceries including a jar of coffee, and we were able to enjoy our first cup in weeks. Later he went to make another when I heard loud swearing. I went to see what was up, and he showed me a now half-empty coffee jar. He opened Fran's cupboard, and sure enough, standing almost alone was a plastic container with half a jar's worth of coffee. He hadn't even tried to hide it.

Various dodgy characters had also started showing up, and I found a used syringe on the kitchen floor (making sense of a lot of stuff including his not eating). I also had £20 disappear from my drawer, which was really not funny. We'd been looking to move out from the start, but there was just nothing we could afford.

As part of our endless quest to stave off boredom, Nick came in from Shepherd's Bush Market one day with two cap gun keyrings he'd bought for a pound each. They didn't look too impressive, until he fired one. The noise was deafening, especially in our bare-walled room.

For the next couple of days we were like a couple of kids, firing them next to the other's ear when they weren't expecting it and inventing various games. One involved setting a wind-up alarm clock a couple of minutes, and whoever fired first after it went off was the winner. It was surprisingly entertaining because you never knew when it would ring, and if your mind wandered even for a second or two, it would slow your reactions and you'd lose.

At some point I went out for a bit, and when Nick heard me come back in, he decided to hide behind the kitchen door to ambush me. He jumped out and fired, only to discover it was Fran who - unbeknown to us - had been going quietly insane from all the cap gun shots coming from our room.

He pinned Nick against the wall and yelled that we had two weeks to move out. When Nick broke the news, we had a huge argument, ending with us both swearing to have nothing more to do with each other.

A few days later I went to meet Paul in a pub on Latimer Road to discuss a derelict house he thought had squatting potential. While waiting for him to show up, I overhead some Irish guy talking about a room he'd just let out. I asked if he happened to have any other places available, and he ended up taking me to the flat he'd just rented out in a block around the corner and offered me the living room. It was another illegal sublet, but only a couple more pounds a week than at Fran's, so I took it.

When Nick found out, he made a grovelling apology and begged me to let him join me. By now the other tenant had decided to move out, so it actually suited me, and I was back to living with my old school enemy.

What seemed like a wonderful stroke of luck proved more a case of 'out of the frying pan...' as Gerry, our new landlord, would end up introducing us to vistas of degradation previously unimagined. I'll spare you the details, but you should get a rough picture if I tell you Nick came in one day to find half a dozen drunks passed out on the carpet and spunk stains on his sheets from where Gerry had fucked someone he described as looking "like a homeless person."

We were there for about six months when Nick got into an argument with Gerry, and for the second time I discovered he'd got us kicked out of a flat that I'd found, followed by another huge row and us both swearing to have nothing more to do with each other. Fate would throw us together once more, though, and this time it was Nick who would come to my rescue, but I might save that story for a later essay.

HOW THE MUSIC INDUSTRY DESTROYED ROCK 'N' ROLL

Tues 3 Oct 2006

I was talking to a friend of my brother's recently about our mutual disillusion with the current music scene.

"I remember when I was a kid," he said, "you'd switch on *Top Of The Pops* and there'd be David Bowie, The Rolling Stones, T Rex, Roxy Music...all these fantastic tracks coming out every week, it seemed. And now...it's almost nothing." (To anyone who thinks music is as good as it's ever been, I suggest comparing a recent chart to one from the '60s or '70s and then ask yourself honestly which set you'd rather take to a desert island.) He asked why I thought this was - as a musician - and if it was simply that the great songs had all been written.

I've heard this idea before, but I don't think creativity really works that way, and between the different notes, rhythms and personalities of the players, there should be a near limitless potential for great music.

I then gave my explanation for the decline which can more or less be blamed on one thing: the music business itself, which is now based around a major label monopoly concerned solely with maximising profits. Couple this with advances in technology that allow literally anyone to sound like a professional artist as well as the increased acceptance of things like on-stage backing tracks, miming, etc., the incentive for labels to seek out and nurture original talent has been markedly reduced, resulting in the dearth of truly memorable and affecting music we are now witnessing.

I added that there probably is some genuinely amazing music being made at the moment, but because of how the industry is structured, the chance of either of us ever hearing it was close to nil.

While the industry has always sought to make money, in the early days studio technology was so basic, with few effects and almost no way to correct a mistake, an artist had to be of a high professional standard just to make a record. The song also had to be well arranged and strong enough to stand up in such an exposed setting. If only from self-interest, labels had to find and develop genuinely talented artists and songwriters, and the most successful ones were usually owned or employed by people like Berry Gordy, Jerry Wexler, Albert Hammond, George Martin, etc. - skilled musicians in their own right and with the ability to recognise talent in its nascent stages.

Promotion was also a more innocent affair back then, often just a matter of mailing a few singles and press sheets to stations and music papers. A large campaign might have stretched to a week or two of press ads. This made for a relatively level playing field where smaller labels could compete, and if a song was good (or at least catchy), it tended to chart, and if not, it flopped.

Juke Box Jury, one of the most popular TV shows of the '50s and '60s (and briefly revived in the '70s), was based on this simple premise, including a panel of artists and industry insiders listening to the latest releases and then voting whether they'd be a "hit" or a "miss." It would be difficult to revive *Juke Box Jury* now, not because of its basic format, but because it would be virtually impossible to predict if a song would be a hit without knowing what was being spent on promotion. In fact, if you knew the budget, you could probably guess without even having to hear it.

That's only a mild exaggeration. In the late '60s, labels started to experiment with full-sized billboard ads and blanket radio campaigns. As they woke up to the power of marketing, it started to become the main focus of the operations, and we're now at the point where as long as the act looks good and the song roughly fits the current scene and isn't completely awful, you can virtually guarantee a Top 40 placing just by spending on promotion. I'm not only referring to obviously manufactured stuff - boy bands, dance acts, etc. This also applies to supposedly credible genres like rock and indie - it just requires a more subtle approach.

Let me show you what I mean by describing how a major label usually launches a new signing.

The first stage of the campaign is what's known as "creating a buzz," basically getting the act's name out there via small reviews, new band features, gossip column mentions, etc. As well as their in-house publicity people, the label will usually hire an independent press person whose job is to schmooze their industry contacts and call in favours.

Press ads are also effective and carry an additional advantage of increasing the chance of being reviewed (and positively) as music papers depend of advertising revenue to stay afloat and will usually do their best to please those paying. I first became aware of this when our manager paid for a couple of ads in *Time Out* and *NME,* and we immediately received our first reviews and suddenly started having our phone calls returned.

Street posters can also help to get the name out. If they're kept to a modest size, they can also lend a subtle credibility to an act due to a romantic image many still hold of the band themselves sticking them up in the middle of the night, perhaps while one of their girlfriends keeps look-out for the cops. If you've ever attempted this, you'll know it's actually not the police you have to worry about as much as the shadey cartels who control the postering business. If one of their guys catches you in the act, expect the threat of violence at the least.

There does need to be some product, usually a low-key single or two (limited edition, vinyl only?), ahead of the album when the real push comes. This is still mainly about establishing the name at this point, so they won't be expecting full hits.

If it's a band, they will be expected to play live, so some showcase gigs or mini-tour will probably be arranged or the label may pay for them to support a more established artist.

You read that correctly. People are often shocked to learn the openers for stadium level acts usually had to pay for the privilege - "buying on" as it's called - assuming they were chosen purely on merit. That used to be the case - in fact, it's how many of the headliners got their first break, but it rarely happens now. Something to consider next time you've forked out half a week's wages to stand at the back of a huge arena drinking over-priced, warm lager from a plastic glass.

Assuming the first stage of the campaign went okay and the band are still talking and haven't developed any major drug problems, the album should soon be ready for release. To sell in any significant quantities usually requires a full chart hit, and for that you need radio play. Even stations like XFM and GLR only allow a couple of their DJs to play what they want, and even that's usually limited to one or two tracks per show. The rest must come from the official playlist which the station programmer compiles each week after meeting with various plugging teams. Most stations won't even consider a track unless it's come via a plugger.

You might wonder why a programmer needs someone else to tell them what to play, especially knowing they're paid to promote them. Mainly it's to filter out the really amateur stuff and also anything that doesn't suit the station's "demographic." The last thing a programmer wants is for people to turn the dial because of one track that's completely different to their tastes. This is why you'll rarely hear a heavy metal song on Radio 1 even if it's already a hit.

Another reason for meeting with pluggers is to hear what kind of marketing campaign the label has planned. The bigger and more targeted to its typical demographic, the more likely they will add it. They may even offer to coordinate plays around the stages of the campaign. So again, the more you spend on advertising, the more additional benefits you gain - in this case airplay.

These days you only have to sell around a thousand copies to make the Top 40, so you'd be unlucky not to have at least made the lower reaches by this point, after which it may gain momentum and start climbing of its own accord. With a chart hit to their name, the label can now ramp things up, with full-page press ads, billboards, etc., and it will simply look like a response to their growing success. Labels are so confident of these strategies, they will often book a new signing into 1,000-plus capacity venues months in advance, knowing that by the time the campaign has run, they'll be able to fill them.

With prohibitive buy-on fees, plugging costs, plus murky deals whereby TV shows, festivals, etc., are only given access to bigger acts on the condition they take on newer signings; the result is a virtual stranglehold where anyone not signed to a major or a major-financed independent is all but barred from competing. In some cases this is explicitly so, e.g., in the US where many radio stations have deals preventing them from playing independent acts during peak listening times.

While this state of affairs would appear to benefit the majors, it's become so expensive to launch an act (half a million is considered average) that it's usually not until their second album they start to recoup their costs - and that's assuming it sells, which is where the system starts to break down. It's one thing persuading people to buy one so-so album, but by the time their next is finished and ready for release, newer, fresher acts will have come onto the scene to compete for their fans' fickle attentions. With the first CD sitting near the bottom of the pile unplayed and unloved for some time, it will require an even harder sell for them to risk burning their fingers a second time.

Rather than continuing to throw good money after bad, labels often cut their losses at this point and simply drop the artist, which is why so many acts disappear not long after their second release. What they'd really like is an act with both wide commercial appeal and longevity, a Blur or U2. But these don't come along every day, so rather than go to endless gigs or sift through endless piles of demos, a quicker, easier option is to poach anyone with promise off the independent labels (who will have done most of the hard work for them) and then use their marketing muscle to break them into the mainstream.

Most independents are run on a shoestring and will usually let an artist go for a reasonable sum. Persuading the act to sign can be more difficult on account of the majors' reputation for creative interference in order to make them as commercial as possible.

To prevent this, their A and R man may offer a "creative control" clause in the contract ensuring no key decisions can be made without the act's consent. These are usually as good as worthless, as should you go against their wishes, all the A and R man has to do is threaten to withdraw promotion (which as we should all know by now will virtually guarantee commercial failure), though being an A and R man he's more likely to phrase it as something like: "While I love your idea of using …. *(insert name of legendary, but currently out-of-vogue producer)* to do the album, rather than ….. *(insert name of flavour-of-the-month producer who makes everyone sound like everyone else that he wants to use),* I'm just not sure I can persuade Marketing to get behind it."

He will then suggest another flavour-of-the-month producer who he insists can get just the sound you're after, but with a slightly more modern twist to appeal to contemporary tastes. If you still refuse, he may hint at terminating your contract (while the artist is tied to the label until they've delivered however many albums are stipulated in the contract, the label can drop you at any time). If he wants to play hard-ball, there's an even nastier weapon in his armoury known as "shelving." This is where they neither release anything nor allow you to leave the deal, meaning you can't even work.

So rather than risk everything over the choice of producer, you concede - telling yourself the occasional compromise is okay if it means being heard by a wider audience. But it won't stop there. Like the descent into prostitution, selling out tends to happen in increments - a tweak of the EQ here, a slightly naff video there. No act awful in itself and each justifiable as part of some greater good, until without knowing precisely how or where, you will have crossed that line and become just another bunch of corporate cock-sucking rock-whores, while your original fans are left wondering how it is bands always seem to end up losing it whenever they sign to a big record company.

Of course, many acts don't mind being told how to sound or look, but for those with a strong or unique vision, having to fight over every decision can be an exhausting and demoralizing experience that ends up sapping them of all their creative energy. From who gets signed to who receives the most promotion, the safe and formulaic are favoured over the innovative, passionate and risk-taking. Aware that labels are mostly looking for more of the same, emerging acts may also start tailoring their music to whatever is currently in fashion, everyone copying what no one was that into in the first place and compounding the problem even further.

Fortunately, great bands still make it through, un-fucked with from time to time, but this should be the norm, not the exception.

Some argue that we are still talking about a business, and on that level at least the majors have been very successful.

But despite the award ceremony back-slapping, the industry is actually in a pretty terrible state right now and continues to be shockingly wasteful (witness the recent £60 million deal given to Robbie Williams). Ironically, most of the majors wouldn't even exist if it wasn't for the revenue coming in from their back catalogues - genuinely great acts signed by people who knew what they were doing and weren't afraid to take risks.

For all its cool pretensions, the music industry is the enemy of great art and the last bastion of Thatcherism.

I only gave my brother's friend a short summary of the above, after which he said, "But isn't that all changing now? What with the internet, MySpace and all of that? Surely bands don't need labels anymore?"

It's true you can now record and release your music without having to be signed, which is brilliant, but because of that there's probably a thousand times as many people now out there calling themselves artists. So unless you're happy mainly being heard by a small circle of friends and relatives, the need for a label is perhaps greater than ever.

And because labels are now using the internet as their way to discover new acts, the ones most likely to get their attention are those either good at self-promotion or with the know-how to draw traffic to their sites, the very people I think we should be trying to discourage, while the true geniuses are languishing in the outer reaches of MySpace with fifteen fans. Because if there's one thing rock history should have taught us, it's that the real greats tend to be a bit dysfunctional and not that at ease with the world, rather than someone with good HTML and organisational skills.

If you think my contempt for the industry is born from bitter personal experience, you're not entirely wrong, but it's not just because of what I've been through.

A couple of years after coming to London, I saw a band I

thought had everything: brilliant musicianship, charisma and, above all, a fantastic set of songs - each one sounded like a hit. I saw them about a dozen times when a notice appeared saying they'd split up without so much as a 7-inch single to their name. They'd done everything a band is meant to do - flyered, postered, gigged extensively, even a couple of publicity stunts.

Had just one label or journalist done what they were supposed to do, I'm convinced they'd have been at least as important as The Smiths. I've seen some other great acts disappear without a trace, and it truly breaks my heart to think how much other incredible music must have been lost to the world.

In Memoriam The Cool Rays.

CHRISTINA AT THE BUS STOP

Wed 4 Oct 2006

After Joe, our original drummer, left the band, we got in Raife, possibly the most sex-obsessed guy I've ever known. He came into rehearsal one day talking excitedly about two blonde girls he'd seen at Tooting Bec station, one of whom he described as 'pure filth' and exactly my type.

The following weekend we were at the HQ Club in Camden when a girl came in who looked like she'd stepped out of a '70s Swedish porno film. As she passed, our eyes locked and she then signalled for me to join her on the dance floor.

"Oh my God!" Raife said, "That's her!! The one I told you about from the tube station!"

She ended up coming back to mine, and we were soon meeting up regularly.

Christina was both physically attractive and great in bed - a rare combination. After one enthusiastic session, I joked that she could make a lot of money doing what she'd just done. She suddenly went serious. "There's something I have to tell you... It's what I do."

In truth, she hadn't done it for a few months, and when she realised I was cool with it, she told me her whole story. She and the other girl Raife saw her with were travelling around Europe for a while when they then ran out of money in Italy. Seeing some street hookers, they thought, *We could do that.*

As the only natural blondes, the punters would usually check them out first, and they were soon making a lot of money. She said they would sometimes bake cookies to give their customers after they'd finished as a treat.

When I asked if she'd had any negative experiences, she smiled and said, "Not really. I don't know what it is - I just love boys!" She really was the archetypal happy hooker.

After coming to London she worked for an escort agency for a while, though she promised herself she'd quit once she found a regular job. She'd since done this, though she'd recently been offered 4 grand for a one-off job with a client, which she admitted she was considering.

We continued to see each other and had some fun times. Once she asked if there were any role-playing fantasies I wanted to try. I suggested an au pair thing, and we arranged an "appointment."

A couple of days later she called to say the cleaning company had sent her and she'd be arriving shortly.

When I opened the door, she was in a full French maid's outfit. Without breaking character she asked which room I wanted her to start in. She then took a feather duster from her bag and started on the skirting board, making sure I got a good view of her cami knickers.

"That picture rail looks quite dusty. I think I'll need to use silk," she said, and then slipped them off.

That was a truly great experience - if a little brief.

Another time we went to a party at the record label we were signed to at the time in Ealing. Some guy was challenging people to down a pint faster than him. She accepted and won. Later, we were waiting to catch a night bus home, and she asked me to fuck her. The stop was right on the High Street and brightly lit, but I wasn't going to say no. I remember some guy passing and doing a massive double take.

A few weeks later I was back at the HQ Club when I happened

to see her snogging another guy. For some reason I could handle her fucking men for money, but seeing her kiss someone purely because she wanted to really pissed me off, and I never called her again.

HOW TO EAT A LIGHT BULB

Thurs 5 Oct 2006

I woke up today with an idea for an essay I planned to call 'My Sister Thinks I'm an Idiot.' She's been very good to me over the years, but I've always suspected that deep down she sees me as this deluded, irresponsible fool yet to outgrow his adolescent pop star fantasies and finally enter the adult world.

I've had similar suspicions of not being taken seriously from other siblings, something I attribute to being the youngest of five. No matter what I do or how old I get, in their eyes I shall always remain the annoying little brother who'd be constantly asking them to explain what was going on in films or bouncing a ball against a wall when they were trying to study for some important exam.

It seems a lot of people have these kinds of issues with family members, be it a parent to whom they are nothing but a source of constant disappointment or maybe their own children who look at them as some pathetic, out-of-touch joke figure. Or it could be the reverse issue to mine, having to always be the responsible one simply because they're the eldest.

So I thought I'd write about this, perhaps ending it by imagining some world-reknowned artist or philosopher having just completed their most ground-breaking work only to find a message from their mum asking if they'd quit their drifting yet and mentioning an office junior position had come up where their friend works and that they might be willing to put in a good word.

But just as I was about to start work, I did something so moronic, it would appear to justify all my sister's worst suspicions.

So what did I do?...I tried to eat a light bulb.

I'm serious. I got as far as chewing the glass and was about to swallow, when I realised the insanity of my actions and began spitting out the bits of broken glass, rinsing and re-rinsing my mouth until I felt it was safe to risk swallowing without ripping apart my internal organs.

But before you start siding with my sister, I'd like to explain the circumstances leading up to this apparent act of insanity, because it wasn't quite as irrational as it sounds.

My story begins four nights ago with a bang from my hallway. I went to investigate, but couldn't see much as for some reason the hallway light had stopped working. There was enough light coming from the living room to see some broken bits of glass on the floor - all of which brought me to the conclusion the bulb had exploded. I don't remember having one physically blow up on me before, but for some reason this one did.

I thought of replacing it, but as there was no bulb to grip onto, I couldn't unscrew the (metal) base without risking electrocution. I thought of switching off the mains power, but then I'd have had no light to see what I was doing, so I decided to leave the problem until the next day and began sweeping up the broken bits of glass so I didn't hurt myself in the meantime.

When I came back to it, I saw that whatever caused the explosion had fused the metal base to the plastic socket part and that I had to replace it. I went to buy a new one from the nearest electrical shop (a couple of miles away), but by the time I'd done that and completed some other chores, it was getting dark again, so I left the problem for another day.

Due to various issues including a wobbly step-ladder and my accidentally cutting the wire too short, requiring another visit to the hardware shop, it wasn't until today I finally got everything sorted and light was restored to my hallway.

I came back this evening to start writing, when I spotted a fairly big bit of broken glass on top of some junk mail by the door, which I'd obviously missed when sweeping up in the semi-light.

I picked it up carefully and was about to drop it in my kitchen bin when I remembered a book I once found among some rubbish on Portobello Road entitled Bed Of Nails. It was the autobiography of a sword-swallower-cum-escapologist known as 'the Amazing Blondini' and turned out to be really interesting. He'd worked in various carnivals and fairs during the 1920s and '30s and described life back then as well as various tricks of the trade. Sword swallowing takes years to master apparently, and many die in the process, including Blondini's own uncle. The bane of every sword-swallower's life are the people in the crowd who shout out that they're obviously using a retractable blade.

He also described the freak shows which were legal then. These were the biggest draws of any fair or carnival, so (contrary to popular opinion) the freaks tended to make big money at a time when a lot of people were starving, and many actually considered themselves blessed. The freaks divided themselves into two groups, the so-called 'naturals' who were born as such and "the self-mades" - normal people who turned themselves into freaks such as 'the blue men' who drank mercury to turn their skin that colour and "the human ostrich" who claimed to eat various household objects including - you guessed it - light bulbs.

Unlike sword swallowing, this is something anyone can do, the secret being to first grind the glass into a fine powder with your back teeth, after which it's safe to swallow - at least according to the Amazing Blondini.

So just as I was about to drop the glass into the bin and thinking what a cool party trick this would make, I decided to give it a go and (as I said) was about to swallow the ground-up powder when common sense made a last second appearance and pointed out I was risking an excruciating death based on the assurance of an excarnie whose book I once found amongst some rubbish.

And now I'm thinking about what would have happened had I swallowed the glass and died as a result – keeping in mind I wouldn't have written any of the above, so no one would know my reasons.

RIDDLE OF LOCAL MAN'S DEATH

Hammersmith and Fulham Gazette, Oct 2006

Police are said to be 'baffled' following the death of local musician Tim Briffa, whose decomposing body was found earlier this week following complaints from neighbours of a 'sickly sweet smell' emanating from his property.

While the cause of death has been attributed to 'massive internal haemorrhaging caused by the ingestion of a small quantity of glass powder', what led him to eat the glass remains a mystery.

"We're still waiting on the coroner's full report," a police spokesman told us yesterday, "but foul play has not been ruled out." He added that Briffa was known for his argumentative nature and may have "rubbed someone up the wrong way."

A couple of weeks later the Gazette would run a follow-up article to say the coroner had declared the case "death by misadventure," and with no evidence of outside involvement having been found, police would now be winding down the investigation.

But that would not be the end of the matter. A staff writer at the *NME* happened to see the article and, recognising my name, submitted a short obituary in which he described My Drug Hell as "indie under-achievers with a small, but loyal, following."

The next issue included a letter from a fan of the band expressing their shock and calling for police to re-open their investigation into the "bizarre circumstances" surrounding my death.

This caught the attention of someone at *Q* magazine who then wrote a small feature entitled "MDH Front Man's Death - The Ten Unanswered Questions."

Over the following months the name My Drug Hell began cropping up more and more in the music press, often accompanied by epithets such as "cult" and "seminal" until it became one of the cool names to drop alongside Neu, Suicide and Can when trying to prove one's hip credentials.

Various rumours and theories started to circulate on how I came to swallow the glass powder - the most persistent being that it was added to some cocaine by a dealer to whom I owed money.

On the back of our growing status, our semi-complete second album was released, padded out with demos and alternate takes. This was followed by a live album recorded at The Bull and Gate pub on a Sony Walkman, and from all this a Greatest Hits collection was somehow cobbled together.

The fact that many of these recordings were of extremely poor quality only seemed to enhance their mystique by lending them an eerie, ghostly quality, until ten years later on the anniversary of my death, a BBC Two Arena documentary on the band would be broadcast. Featuring contributions from various ageing indie stars including Jarvis Cocker and a greying Noel Gallagher, it concluded with its own investigation into my passing, managing to track down the pathologist who'd conducted the original autopsy.

It was quick to scotch the cocaine dealer/murder theory and an even more scurrilous one involving the underage daughter of the Chief of the Hammersmith Police, but ultimately remained inconclusive.

The documentary ended with an interview with "former bassist and close personal friend" David Preston. Looking tanned and healthy by the pool of his LA mansion, he gave his own theory on the cause of my death - a simple suicide. He talked about my bouts of self-doubt and depression, though when asked why I'd chosen such an agonising and unreliable method, admitted he wasn't sure.

As the camera pulls back, we see Dave's model girlfriend dive gracefully into the water, the ripples fading artfully to a shot of me looking fresh faced from my younger days, over which the narrator solemnly intones, "While we may never know how the world was robbed of one of its finest talents, of one thing we can be certain: the music of My Drug Hell shall live for many years to come."

Cue credits and, predictably, 'Girl at the Bus Stop.' (Don't TV producers have any imagination?)

AIMS, AMES AND AMIE

Fri 6 Oct 2006

I had a call earlier from an Australian girl I've known for a little while called Amie. I'm not sure how to describe our relationship. I'd say we're friends, but we sometimes have sex, which friends aren't meant to do. "Fuck buddies" doesn't feel right either, as to me that suggests people who meet primarily to have sex, then maybe hang out for a bit after, whereas we meet primarily to hang out and then sometimes have sex if we get bored of talking. Everything we do seems to be a kind of default option. She even told me, "You know the only reason I'm only sleeping with you is because I can't find anyone better right now?"

I think what attracts me to her most is that she can make me laugh, which not that many women can do, I'm sorry to say. She's also rare in almost never talking about emotional or relationship-type stuff. She said an ex-boyfriend once accused her of having a "wall around her heart." I've never probed for possible explanations, though a couple of bricks came down one time when she alluded to some dark stuff involving another ex- boyfriend in Australia which was the main reason she moved here.

We haven't really talked the last week. I called a couple of days ago, but she sounded distant, and when I asked if everything was okay, she replied, "Not really," and then said she had to go. I sent a text back asking what was wrong, but she didn't reply until the next day and still wouldn't say.

Whatever the reason, it sounded quite serious as when I spoke to her today I heard her start to cry for the first time. She immediately apologised and changed the subject by asking how these essays are going. (It was Amie who lent me *I Love You More Than You Know*, the book by Jonathon Ames that inspired me to start them.)

Had she asked this a few days ago or even earlier last night, I'd probably have said they were going well - I might even have said "very well." But then something happened last night that completely took the wind out of my sails.

I was speaking to a friend about the essays on the phone. He's normally very encouraging with my creative projects, but instead of saying, "You've got some good stories; I can imagine it being really good," or whatever I was secretly hoping to hear, he came out with this really muted response, asking if I thought there'd be an audience for such a thing. I might have handled it had I not had an almost identical reaction a couple of days before from someone else who is close to me, who then asked how easy it would be to find a publisher.

Though neither was trying to be negative, I could tell they both thought it was a little arrogant for someone like me to be writing a book about my life, opinions, etc., which I can totally understand. No one has commissioned me to write this, and it's not like I'm some massive rock star. I'm a complete nobody as far as most people are concerned.

I told them both about Jonathan Ames, that I didn't think his life was any more interesting than mine and that anyone could write a good book as long as they knew what to focus on, but having to justify myself for the second time in a few days sent me into this huge mental tailspin about myself and the whole project.

Because the fact is I don't know if anyone will be interested or what people will make of it if I do find a publisher (something I hadn't even thought about until it got mentioned). For all I know, all I'm doing by writing this is hanging myself with my own rope - immortalising myself as this deluded, self-important twat, while letting the entire world know my innermost secrets and insecurities.

I also started having doubts about some of the essays themselves. I'd just finished the one about eating the light bulb, which I had been quite pleased with. But then I remembered one by Jonathan Ames about trying to kill a cockroach, and while I really did try to eat the bulb, etc., I thought I might have subconsciously ripped off his style.

The stuff about becoming posthumously famous reminded me of another essay of his where he says he still fantasises about becoming a pro basketball player, even though he's in his forties and clearly hasn't a chance. In his case it works, because he's already a successful writer, and it's obviously written for comic effect, but making it in music isn't a joke for me. It's pretty much all I've wanted since I was twelve.

That, plus some of the other jokey essays, made me think I was creating this cartoon version of myself as this slightly wacky character, forever getting into scrapes with various women, all the while labouring under the hilarious delusion I might one day make it as a rock star.

And at the risk of sounding even more deluded, if it hadn't been for all the shit we went through with labels going bust, members leaving, etc., I think we would be well known by now, perhaps even deserving of our own BBC documentary.

It's probably because of how painful that stuff was that I sometimes make light of it now. You can tell a story in many different ways, and if I wanted, I could talk about how it feels knowing you have everything it takes to make truly great music while barely being able to operate for years at a time, and it would be one of the most depressing things you've ever read. There was a particularly bleak couple of years when I was also getting over an extremely fucked-up relationship situation, and it was a struggle just to get out of bed. It was like I was in this long, dark tunnel, not knowing if I'd ever find a way out.

I managed to eventually, thank Christ, and now that I'm at the point where I can actually joke about it, it's made me aware of what an incredible thing humour is - not just as a way of dealing with all the shit, but to transform it into something that can make yourself and others feel good. It really is a form of alchemy.

I suspect a lot of people who joke around a lot are renegades from some dark side, which is maybe why Amie also likes her silly, trivial stuff.

I told her my worry that I was turning myself into this 2D caricature and added that I do actually have a serious side.

"Oh, I know you do," she said. "I've seen it. But I prefer the funny you to the serious you."

By the end of the conversation, we were both starting to joke a bit, and she told me a funny story about walking in on a flatmate who was masturbating to the MTV Dance Channel.

Though we hadn't solved each other's problems, we'd cheered each other up a little, enough hopefully to last until some brighter day. And by writing this, it's reminded me there's a place in this world for a bit of idiocy, and if that means talking about posthumous Arena documentaries and sounding a bit of a twat sometimes, then so be it.

After writing all this, I remembered another essay by Jonathan Ames where he'd just broken up with some girl, realises he's just this lonely old guy and ends up sobbing for about an hour. It's pretty depressing, but interesting too, as you see this whole other side to him. So I appear to have ripped him off again!

And now I've remembered he ends that essay by mentioning a depressing, but revealing, passage in someone else's book. I shall remain calm.

DIRTY NEEDLES AND THE HATCHAM SOCIAL CLUB

Sat 7 Oct 2006

I have a guy called Toby moving in with me shortly for a couple of weeks. I met him at the Notting Hill Arts Club when his band the Hatcham Social played recently. I only caught the end of their set, but I liked it and went up to say so. I also had a hunch we'd get on, which seemed born out as we spent the rest of the night getting drunk together, talking about music and trying (and failing) to chat up two Japanese girls.

At some point I asked where he lived. He said he'd spent the previous few weeks sleeping on a friend's kitchen floor and then asked if I knew of any rooms going. I said I had one myself, but an old tenant was about to take it again.

"Even just for a week or two would be amazing," he said.

I said to call me when I was sober and had a chance to think about it. A few days later he rang, and I asked what he could afford to pay.

"I dunno...maybe £20?"

"A week?" I said this would barely cover bills.

"I could maybe go to...25." He sounded pained.

I said to give me a bit of time to think, but before hearing back I ran into him again at the Arts Club. He didn't mention the room, but I asked if he was still on the kitchen floor, and he said he was. This was just after I'd written the essay about coming to London which had reminded me of how often I'd narrowly avoided homelessness (there were some other times when I ended up squatting for a while) as well as how fortunate I am no longer to have to worry about that stuff.

That plus the parallels between his situation now and mine then (young, broke musician hoping to make it in London), and the fact I'd felt compelled to speak after his gig, felt too much to ignore - as if the Universe was conspiring to ensure I took care of him by reminding me of all the times it had come to my aid. So I said he could have the room at the original £20 (a fiver's not going to make much difference). It's a bit of risk as I don't really know him, but it felt right and I think it will be fine.

I had the urge to go up to another guy at a club in Bloomsbury a few weeks ago. I didn't know what to say, but he looked like a musician, so I ended up going, "So what's your band called?" He laughed and then told me they'd only recently got together and yet thought of a name. "How about The Comedowns?" I said (a name I thought of recently).

"Hmm, not sure... It's not bad, though."

"What about The Dirty Needles?" (another one I was toying with. I seem to be stuck on a theme).

"The Dirty Needles?" He said to himself a couple of times. "You know, I actually quite like that. I'll have to run it by the others."

I said if they did use it they'd have a good story for their bio or for any journos who asked how they got it. ("This guy just came up and asked what the name of the band was...")

At the end of the night he asked my number, and a couple of days later I got a text: "Feller, the name went down a storm!! The more I say it, the more it rocks!" They've since set up a MySpace page under the name.

I've found stuff like this happens a lot when following hunches, and rather than a load of random, meaningless events, life takes on a fiction or movie-like feel - if not yours, then you become a player in someone else's or the big Cosmic one. I don't remember anything bad happening as a result, and I've also made some good friends through it. Now I've said that, Toby will probably turn out to be a complete nightmare and I'll come back to find the locks changed and my stuff on the street - that really would be karma.

HOW TO PICK UP GIRLS Pt. 2

Sun 8 Oct 2006

Whenever it comes up I've written a play called *How to Pick Up Girls* it's usually just a matter of time before the question comes, "...and so how *do* you pick up girls?"

My standard response is to say, "I only wish I knew," and then remind them it was a work of fiction, but in truth it's a subject I've given a lot of thought to over the years, and if they seem genuinely interested, I'm usually happy to offer a theory or two.

It's not just men who ask me this question, though if it's coming from a girl, it's usually accompanied by a slight narrowing of eyes and crossing of arms and offered mainly to prove they would never be so dumb as to fall for some kind of set routine or "shtick." Women are quick to tell you how easy it is to get a man to do what they want, but suggest they can also be played, and they're invariably outraged.

But just because I think it's possible to manipulate a girl into bed doesn't mean I agree with it, and I generally try to avoid direct game-playing. So instead of this being a set of pulling tricks I've been told about or witnessed being used as I originally intended, I've decided to make it a more general overview of the subject which I'm hoping will be less open to abuse.

Before I start, there's something I need to make absolutely clear which is that men and women are not the same. That might be obvious to most people, but every now and again I run into someone who believes the old school Feminist/PC notion that our differences are purely the result of social conditioning, girls being given dolls to play with and boys being given guns, etc., plus a culture that praises a guy who sleeps around while putting down a woman who does the same.

Conditioning certainly has a major effect, but we would behave differently regardless of the culture we are raised in due to a range of hormonal, cognitive and biological differences governing perception and sexuality, many of which can be observed long before conditioning could have had any significant effect. (At just six hours of age, baby girls react more keenly to sounds. At six months they are better at recognizing faces, while boys of the same age have better spatial awareness skills.)

The most significant difference is that only one of the sexes can become pregnant. This influences the traits we seek in a potential partner as well as inclining the woman more towards monogamy than the male who can potentially father dozens of children in the time it takes her to produce one.

It matters not whether we consciously want or even like children. After ensuring our own survival on this planet, our strongest instinct is to pass on our DNA via the fittest specimen we think we can attract so that one day it can do the same - the perpetuation of our species. This is what all the flirting, buying drinks and asking what bands the other person is into is ultimately all about.

Not only is the idea of the sexes being the same demonstrably false, but rather than bringing us together, I believe it's created even bigger divisions, and it's only by accepting we have different desires and drives that we have any hope of understanding one another and truly getting on.

So unless anyone has any questions? No one? Good. Then I'll begin.

1. PRIMARY CHARACTERISTICS WOMEN SEEK –
   PROVIDER/PROTECTOR

Babies require almost constant attention. To raise one alone in primitive times - where we've spent the vast bulk of our evolution – would have meant an increased risk for both mother and child of dying from hunger, thirst, exposure, etc.

It is therefore etched deep into every woman's subconscious to avoid indiscriminate sex, lest she fall pregnant as a result, and, where possible, to seek out the best provider/protector she can find. Once this would have meant someone resourceful and/or physically strong, but tends now to translate as someone successful/wealthy or with the makings of success. So any outward signs of this (fast car, expensive suit, Rolex, etc.) is guaranteed to draw female attention.

It's no use him being rich if he later runs off (which wealthy men are more likely to do by virtue of their popularity), so he must also appear sincere in his intentions, so any form of romantic display (flowers, poetry, etc.) or a willingness to commit (a ring on the finger being the ultimate) will also elicit a strong response.

Ideally, she'd like a man who is both rich and in love, but luckily for most guys, women will usually accept a shortfall in the wealth department if the man shows sufficient passion on the basis that what he lacks in resources he should make up for in his willingness to stick around and work hard on behalf of her and any future offspring.

It follows from this that one of the worst things a man can show a woman is a lack of passion. Like a lot of guys, when I first started going on the pull, I'd chat up as many women as I could, thinking I was increasing my chances - the "throw as much mud..." approach. This can work in some situations, but in a closed environment like a club, you're often shooting yourself in the foot. If she's at all interested in you, she'll have been checking you out too (if less obviously), and if she's had to watch you try it on with half a dozen girls before getting around to her, you've as good as told her you won't be sticking around.

Other ways to signal your general half-heartedness is to forget her name shortly after being given it or to continue scanning the room while talking to her. Simple stuff, you'd think, but it's amazing how many guys make these elementary mistakes.

The above constitute the primary characteristics a woman looks for in a man, roughly equivalent to what appearance and sexuality represent to men. It's worth noting that the physical traits men are most drawn to (full lips, firm breasts, curves, etc.) are all indicators of fertility so ultimately still relate to reproduction and the creation of healthy offspring. It's also been shown that good-looking people are trusted more and tend to do better in life, so beauty also confers a survival advantage.

2. SECONDARY CHARACTERISTICS – LOOKER, LOVER, ENTERTAINER

The more choice a woman has, the more she can look towards finding someone who satisfies her on a more personal level.

A glance through any lonely hearts column shows the most universally sought male personality trait is a "GSOH." It's unclear why women find humour such a turn-on.

Similar to an orgasm, being made to laugh is an involuntary, yet pleasurable reflex - so there could be a subconscious link to that. Or it might simply be that so few women can tell a joke, when they find someone who can do so without screwing up the punch-line, they'll sleep with them out of gratitude.

Humour also suggests the man is intelligent as well as "safe" and not some psycho who won't take "no" for an answer. It's easy for men to overlook how threatening they are potentially to a woman, and rightly or wrongly psychopaths are assumed to be intense individuals not given to making light-hearted quips the whole time.

Though not as high a priority as for most men, she does still need to feel physically attracted. Sexual prowess is also important, but with no way of knowing how a man will perform in bed without actually sleeping with him - something she's programmed to keep to a minimum - she may rely on more subtle indicators of his abilities according to her personal preferences, which is why women can be aroused by something as seemingly abstract as an athletic performance or even a passionate piano recital.

Every woman is different, and some may be more typically male in their desires, but for the most part it seems nature has given her the task of caring for the child and for the man to make sure it's not too ugly.

3. VETTING METHODS

Being attracted primarily to appearance, it's easy for a man to know who is a candidate for his attentions, but as all the main traits a woman looks for (wealth, power, desire for commitment, safety, etc.) are either not apparent from appearance or can be faked or lied about, how does she know who is worth fluttering her eyelashes at and working her subtle magic on?

One way is by checking the women around him. A hot babe on your arm is like a great reference on a CV. She won't know what's attracting her (Great in bed? Heir to a fortune?), but she will assume it's good and worth having.

Of course this is of limited use if he's already with someone. A more useful sign he has something going for him is confidence, which is why almost every self-help book recommends it, though he might simply be full of himself.

Probably the most reliable way to know if a guy is genuine and not some loser/chancer hoping for an easy lay is by simply holding off before having sex. This seems to come more naturally to women who on average feel most in the mood for sex around the third to fifth date. If anything, men are inclined to lose interest the longer they've known the person, which can present a problem as by the time she is finally in the mood, he may be going off the idea.

Should he proceed despite his waning interest, there is another potential hurdle in the form of a chemical women produce after having sex called oxytocin - aka the "cuddling" or "bonding" hormone - making her feel even more attached.

Having spent several nights getting to know him (or as she will see it "investing in the relationship"), he can no longer expect to leave with a peck on the cheek and a "See you around sometime." Floating in a sea of oxytocin and thinking about her next fix, she will want to know precisely when she will next see him around, and should he feel forced to offer a date, will then be asked why it can't be sooner.

By the time he's extricated himself from the situation, he'll have paid such a high price in term of DVDs starring Renee Zellweger and increasingly needy phone calls, he'll think a lot more carefully before pulling that stunt again.

So again, what appears to be a huge evolutionary cock-up proves a great way to reduce babies born to unsuited couples and another victory for Mother Nature.

Women's reluctance to jump into bed may partly be learned behaviour, but it also has a physiological basis. While the area of the male brain that processes sexual thoughts is located in both hemispheres, for women it's predominantly located in just one. So while he is in a kind of permanent sexual standby, able to turn his thoughts to sexual matters almost regardless of what he is focussed on, the woman tends to require some "warming up." When it comes to processing emotions, it's women who use both halves and men who employ one and require the "warming up."

If this one fact was better known, I believe it would do more to bring the sexes together than the entire works of Feminism combined. No longer would women have to puzzle over how her man can be warm and loving one day and cold and distant the next. Nor would men wonder how their partner could be asking him to talk dirty one night, then storming out the next because he suggested a quickie.

It also means that whether one is looking for love or sex, one should heed the lesson of "frog boiling," namely, if you turn up the heat too fast, it will jump out.

4. BASTARDS

From everything I've talked about, it would seem like the ideal man would be romantic, sensitive, charming, etc., yet we've all known men who are none of these things, yet attract more women than almost anyone.

Bastards, as they're commonly known, break all the known laws of pulling. Instead of wooing a girl with flowers and candlelit dinners, he's more likely to invite her to some dive bar where he'll get her to pay for the drinks before shagging her in the alleyway around the back. He'll then ignore her calls until a couple of weeks later when he sends a text saying to come straight to his wearing her best lingerie - which she'll spend five minutes cursing, before ordering a cab.

Even women struggle to explain the appeal of the exact type they should be running a mile from. But it's actually not so irrational, as indirectly bastards fit almost all the criteria they are programmed to seek.

By refusing to follow the standard rules of seduction, this suggests an alpha male/ leader type, thus marking him as a good potential provider. His unpredictability tends to make him exciting to be around - ticking the "good entertainer" box. His overt sexuality is usually passionate, another plus, and the fact he's so upfront about his desires ironically suggests a certain honesty that some find refreshing, given most guys are looking for sex, but try to hide it.

The only area he falls seriously short in is commitment. Yet even this can work to his advantage. Given the human tendency to project, she will likely attribute this to some past emotional hurt which only her unique form of loving can cure.

By the time she's realised he's not some wounded soul and really is just a bastard, he'll have slept with half her friends and moved on to pastures new.

5. THE EVOLUTIONARY LOOPHOLE

Non-bastards might now be wondering if there's any way to get a girl into bed without having to somehow subvert their desire for something long term. "What about nymphomaniacs?" I hear you all ask. "Do they really exist? And if so, where can I meet them?"

Nymphos do exist. But they are usually nuts and more trouble than they're worth. This is an observation, not a value judgement, and not surprising when you consider the dangers and lack of biological advantage for a woman to have a multitude of anonymous partners.

Fortunately, there are some relatively sane women who enjoy sex for its own sake from time to time. I refer to this idea in my play, where I call it the "1 in 10 Rule" – being the approximate proportion of women who have the same attitude to sex as most men. To quote Ted Dellar, the US sex guru whose CD course gives the play its name, "This doesn't just mean one in ten women feel the same way as you, but the remaining nine out of ten women feel the same way as men one-tenth of the time."

By learning to recognize who is genuinely up for it, much of the game-playing can be avoided. This is more of a "vibe" thing (which I will come to later). Suffice to say it's often the opposite of who one might expect (when picking out potential groupies, Beatle roadies were instructed to go for "the quiet ones at the back"). In the same way that men use the promise of romance to procure sex, it can also be confused by the fact that women will often play up their sexuality to get what they want - be it a relationship, a confidence boost or just a night of free drinks.

She may not be deliberately leading you on. One way alcohol affects women is to temporarily raise their testosterone levels, making them feel more 'male' sexually, usually reverting to type a bit later in the night, when the genuinely horny ones have usually left with someone.

6. THE MAGIC FORMULA

I said at the start I'm against direct game-playing; however, there's one technique I've used and can't resist talking about.

I discovered/developed it a few years ago with Raife (the sex-obsessed drummer I mentioned in the 'Christina at the Bus Stop' essay), and it involves some of the principles I've discussed. In fact, it's how I figured many of them out.

At the time we'd become friends with Grub Smith who wrote a column called 'The Laboratory Of Love' for FHM in which he'd often road-test some technique or toy. As a result he'd get sent a lot of invites to things likes sex exhibitions or launch parties for some new condom range, which he told us were usually full of semi-naked models and Page 3 types. He'd been in the job long enough to have grown bored with all of this, so we began pestering him for any press passes he wasn't planning to use.

The first we went to was a birthday party for Live TV, the UK's first porn channel, famous at the time for showing topless darts. As promised there were various scantily clad women about, who we spent most of the night ogling and being ignored by. Eventually, we did what we often did when we'd given up on a club or party and retreated to a corner to talk music, tell jokes, etc. (Raife can be very funny, so we'd usually end up in hysterics.)

After about twenty minutes, two model types introduced themselves. Girls often came up when we "withdrew" like this, curious as to why we weren't acting like everyone else or perhaps just wanting to get in on our good time, but we weren't expecting it to happen somewhere like this.

Then a couple more girls came over, and by the end of the night we'd been given three or four phone numbers including that of their Swedish (topless) weather presenter and one of the leads from their erotic soap opera 'Threesome.' I should mention that Raife never took advantage of these offers as he had a girlfriend who he was very much in love with. I never quite understood what he got out of chatting up hot women he could never sleep with, but he seemed to enjoy the flirting and said he got a kick out of turning them down at the end of the night.

The next invite, more or less the same thing happened. Shortly after retreating to a quiet corner, a girl came over and asked if we were in a band. Raife was in the middle of some story, so he just went, "Yeah, we are," and continued talking. She then asked the name. Raife replied that she wouldn't have heard of us, which was probably true, but rather than give up, it seemed to make her more curious, and she began insisting we were famous. She called her friend over, saying we were in some famous band, which Raife then started playing to by still refusing to give our name.

At some point the second girl tried to kiss him. He pushed her away going, "Leave me alone," which again made her even more persistent. As we got drunker, he became increasingly outrageous, telling her at one point that he wouldn't have sex with her, but would consider coming in her face. He often came out with this crude, but funny stuff with girls in clubs. They'd usually push him or act mock-outraged, but they'd almost always stick around and often come onto him later. But with these girls the effect seemed magnified tenfold, and he ended up with both of them all over him. Later he got talking to a lingerie model who handed him her card with a note saying, "Call me. Day or Night."

Later we tried making sense of all of this. We already knew the reason girls like it when you're rude or dismissive is because it suggests you have something going for you (similar to why they find confidence or bastards attractive), but it's one thing treating a regular club-goer like she's beneath you; to do this to some stunning model suggests you must really be something special – and hence the girl's insistence we were famous.

Once we'd figured out the psychology, we began to apply it, and by about the fifth event we had it down to a set of precise moves: After entering the room, we'd go straight to the bar without even glancing at any of the girls no matter how beautiful or how little they were wearing. We'd continue to talk and look only at one another.

Within about forty minutes we'd start to notice a few girls gravitating towards us in our periphery vision, until eventually one would come up and say something, e.g., "How are you guys doing?" to which we'd give the briefest answer, "Good, thanks," and carry on our conversation. She'd either become more persistent or walk off slightly dazed at having received her first brush-off in years/ever.

If she did walk off, someone a bit braver (who would likely have witnessed this) would give it a go, and at some point we'd drop the cool act and properly engage in the evening, though continuing to make no effort to be polite (e.g., not offering to buy them a drink) and being as rude/crude as we felt.

The worse we behaved, the more they'd react, which would draw the attention of other girls, until we'd sometimes have a little crowd caught up in this incredible filth feedback loop, and all of it based on bluff. (Can you see why I named it "the Magic Formula"?)

We had some mad nights. I remember looking at Raife with three models around him, suddenly grabbing his nose and going,

"Did one of you just fart?" Another time a well-known porn model bet him £20 she'd fuck him by the morning. Raife won (if you can call not fucking a porn model "winning").

Raife was always better at this stuff than me, maybe because he wasn't trying to have sex, whereas I'd usually betray my intentions by coming on too soon or taking the bad boy stuff a little too far (probably shouldn't go into that). I didn't usually care if I blew it as we'd usually have had so much fun by that point. I remember leaving one place laughing our heads off while Raife threw four or five phone numbers into the gutter, going, "Idiots!"

7. CHEMISTRY/ENERGY

Having since read *The Game* - Neil Strauss' account of the US pick-up scene, I can see what we were doing was like an extreme version of what he calls "the Neg" - where you make a subtle put-down in order to suggest "high value."

While I enjoyed the book, I was surprised he never discussed chemistry, as if as long as a girl looks good, she's worth pursuing. In my experience not only is it much harder to pull someone if there's no chemistry, but the sex will be terrible even if you succeed.

I once met a Spanish girl with whom I felt instant chemistry. We went back to hers, and were soon meeting up every weekend. What was unusual about this was that neither of us could speak more than four or five words of the other's language. It was about three weeks before I worked out she'd come here to study, yet I never felt bored, and we'd be constantly laughing our heads off as we tried to communicate by pulling faces and pointing at things.

As her English improved (obviously I made no attempt to learn her language), we were able to have more in-depth conversations and began to properly get to know each other. It turned out we had quite a lot in common - she even shared my contempt for

Feminism, which was rare back then, and we continued seeing each other for another two or three years.

It occurred to me later this might just as easily have killed the relationship - she could have been some Franco-supporting fascist for all I knew. What was also interesting is that it didn't significantly improve things either. We still spent about the same amount of time together, and I wouldn't say we had any better time than when our only way of communicating was through sign language.

Most people think the reason we get on with some people and not others is because we have shared interests, but this and other stuff I'd learned through practising meditation brought me to the conclusion that every living thing has its own unique energy field or "frequency," some of which "harmonise" with our own, making us feel good to be around and stimulating thoughts, humorous ideas, etc., while others create a dissonance, putting us on edge and making it harder to articulate ideas, be funny, etc.

Although the people we get on with do often have similar tastes, this isn't why we get on as much as a reflection of compatible energies which draw us to similar interests, artists, etc. While energy levels may fluctuate, our basic "frequency" is fixed, which is why our relationship with people we've known for many years tends to be very similar no matter how much we feel we've changed outwardly.

Even animals react to these energies which is why they sometimes form both "friends" with whom they go everywhere with and "enemies" that they constantly fight with.

Sexual chemistry is also a reflection of how our energies combine, and because it's all a manifestation of the same thing, I believe you can predict with a fair degree of accuracy how you will get on sexually by how you relate on a conversational level.

To do this, one has to ignore the topic of discussion and focus instead on the overall dynamic. If the conversation flows easily without any awkward silences, most likely you'll stay interested in the bedroom. If you have to force the conversation or find it hard to concentrate on what they're saying, the sex will probably also feel like work. If the conversation is light, but the silences aren't embarrassing, the sex will probably be good, if a bit lacking in fireworks. If the discussion sometimes gets heated, but you find it interesting, things are likely to be more passionate.

You can get quite specific on this. If you find yourself getting on like a house on fire the first time you meet, but the next it's like you've said everything you have to say - that would probably have been a great one-night stand (though that ship will probably now have sailed). If the conversation seems to go round in circles without ever reaching any satisfying conclusion, that too will be mirrored in bed (if you get my meaning).

There must still be a physical attraction, but ultimately it's the person's energy we are drawn to and does or doesn't maintain our interest.

8. LOVE

Occasionally one feels an attraction that is so strong it is to good chemistry what heroin is to cannabis, complete with opiate-like highs when together and withdrawal-like symptoms when apart. Cynics sometimes attribute such relationships (aka "true" love) to a kind of desperation or "settling" issue, yet even the rich and famous with almost limitless choice will often have that one person they can't seem to walk away from.

As if put together by some cosmic matchmaker, the attraction is so strong and mutual, it's like you couldn't mess up if you tried. If you make a clumsy pass, she will find it endearing; if you have some spinach between your teeth, she will say, "Oh my God, you like spinach too? I thought I was the only one!"

But even true love has its ups and downs and doesn't necessarily work out, in which case it can be devastating. Some mystics believe falling in love is a way to work out karma from a previous lifetime, and what better way to have to resolve your differences than literally be addicted to them? Whatever the cause, it's an awesome and powerful force.

9. BREAKING UP

If you are on the pulling or dating scene long enough, chances are you will eventually end up with someone who is more into the relationship than you, forcing you to break up with a person you may like, just not quite enough to sacrifice your independence for.

I've asked a few girls how to end a relationship, and they've all said it's easy: just tell the other person straight - it's not giving you what you need and you can't do it any more. I suspect the reason they say it's easy is because for them it usually is. If you tell a man it's over, he'll probably feel upset, but once he's established it's not some bluff, he'll then retreat to some dark mental place for however many months or years it takes before he's ready to go back out there and risk having it all happen again.

But ending it with a woman is a whole other thing. Usually her first reaction is to go into pragmatic mode, asking precisely what you're unhappy with and then offering a range of possible solutions - most of them involving spending more time together. If you insist nothing can save it, she will then enter full-on emotional mode, at which point almost anything can happen. She may kick, scream, throw stuff and call you every name under the sun, but by far and away the hardest to deal with is when she starts to cry.

When at last the tears stop, you are still only at the very start of the process and can expect several months of calls and texts, alternating between saying how much she misses you and telling you what a bastard you are. At some point she'll say she never wants to speak to you ever again, only to ring a few hours later accusing you of being an even bigger bastard for not checking she was okay.

Until one day the calls stop for real, which can only mean one thing. She has found someone else who, should you be foolish enough to ask, has all the qualities you lacked before adding she now realises it wasn't you she loved, but the "idea" of you which was basically what you'd told her at the start.

Okay, so maybe now I'm the one projecting. Still, when women say men are afraid of relationships, I think it's not the relationship most of us fear, but how it will end.

10. THE RULE THAT MEANS YOU DON'T NEED RULES/INSTINCTIVE APPROACH

Men hoping to glean tips from all of this may by now be feeling confused. While it seems some women want a man who is charming and sensitive, others prefer a more rough-and-ready type. To make matters worse, the same woman may be attracted to a different type at different points in her life, or even from one day to the next. (A recent study showed women were more attracted to photos of guys on motorbikes during the middle of their menstrual cycle.)

However, there is a way of knowing who wants what – by using one's instinct/intuition. Instinct will tell you who is looking for love, who wants sex, when to be crude and how crude you can get away with being. Instinct knows everything, and everyone has it, so it's worth getting in touch with.

In its basic form, instinct is like a glorified "yes/no" system, so if you want to develop yours, the first thing to do is to recognise one from the other. If you ever told a joke that bombed, most likely you knew just before telling it that it was inappropriate or the wrong moment. That was your instinct saying "no."

You may also have felt this when meeting someone who later

proved untrustworthy. For me it's almost a physical tightening in the chest, but it may be less specific.

The "yes" feeling is really just an absence of the "no" feeling. Like a bell ringing true, everything inside feels relaxed and at ease.

A good way to start applying one's instinct is first to enter the relaxed "yes" state – saying and doing only what feels comfortable, without forcing anything. Then any time you get that slightly tense "no" feeling, stop what you were about to say or do, wait until you're back in the relaxed "yes" state and then continue. Instinct only works in the present tense, so it's possible whatever you were about to say or do may still be appropriate at a later time.

Once you're familiar with the two feelings, you can make decisions by contemplating a question and waiting for the response.

"Should I go up to the brunette at the bar? No? Okay, how about the blonde in the corner?...Great, she seems nice."

This doesn't mean she'll sleep with you, but it should at least be a positive experience and you'll enjoy the conversation.

Because instinct can be such a subtle voice, they can easily be drowned out by our two other primary drives, that of "Logic" (intellectual, "rational" thought, etc.) and "Animal" (lust, emotions, fear, etc.).

Like a skilled barrister, Logic can be very convincing when presenting its case. "So you're thinking about chatting up the blonde, are you? And what makes you think she'd be interested in you? Oh, you have a *feeling,* do you? Get real. You're not remotely in her league."

Animal can also be persuasive when trying to satisfy its needs. "Forget the blonde. It's the brunette you should be going for. Trust me, she's well dirty. Who cares if you're getting a dodgy vibe - live a little!"

So you go for the brunette, and it seems Animal was right. Until just as you get to hers, she gets a call from an ex saying he's on his way over. As you find yourself stuck in the middle of nowhere at 4am, you finally get what your instinct was trying to tell you.

Instinct doesn't only apply to seduction. It can be used to make any decision: where to move to, what job to take, what car to buy, anything, though it's particularly useful in situations where you don't have all the information or when dealing with strangers.

As well as its subtlety, people often ignore their instinct because it means having to abandon a comfortable, familiar situation in favour of an unpredictable one with no guarantee of success. For example, it may tell you to give up your secure, well-paid job in order to start your own business. And the business may still fail. However, the wisdom usually becomes apparent in time - the failed business teaches you some lesson that proves crucial in setting up another that is a success. Or it leads you to another line of work you wouldn't have considered otherwise but are much happier in. So ultimately, you never regret following it.

Instinct is a genius of lateral thinking, providing solutions not even Logic could devise, and if you do ignore it, it won't hold a grudge. You can ask for advice at any time, and it will do everything it can to get things back on track or make the best of a difficult situation. It really is the wisest and kindest friend you could ask for, unlike those fair-weather ones Animal and Logic.

I seem to have strayed from the initial brief here. Anyway, develop your instinct and you can pretty much forget everything else I've said.

(This essay was expanded on after its initial writing. See also 'End Notes.')

BUSKERS WILL BE PROSECUTED

Mon 9 Oct 2006

I ran into a film-maker friend called Helen earlier who was complaining she can't work at the moment as she has to do jury service. One of my brothers did this. Like her, it was only for a week or two, but he said if you were put onto something like a big fraud case, it could last months. That could be a disaster for me if we had a tour or recordings, so I came up with an idea to get off it by sending a letter saying something like this:

> "Dear Crown Prosecution Service,
>
> While I would love to carry out jury duties as requested, I should warn you that as a practising Buddhist who doesn't believe in the concept of guilt, my religious conscience prevents me from passing anything apart from a verdict of "not guilty". I hope that won't be a problem.
>
> Yours sincerely…"

No doubt whoever opened it would suspect it was a ruse, but they couldn't be certain. Would they want to risk the possible collapse of some case months in the preparation because of one jury member? And for it then to maybe come out he'd actually written a letter informing them of his intentions - only for some fool to ignore it? I reckon most would play it safe and at the least avoid assigning them to anything serious.

I think you can often beat the system if you use a lateral approach and can make yourself a big enough potential pain in the arse.

A friend was driving at high speed down a back street in Kensington when the police waved him down. He decided to ignore them, but they managed to get his number, and a few days later he received a summons. He hired a good lawyer who pointed out the charge was only for failing to stop, not the actual speeding, and advised him to say the reason he kept driving was because he was going so fast, it would have been dangerous to suddenly apply the brakes!

It reminded me of when George Harrison was sued for taking the melody of The Chiffons' 'He's So Fine' for 'My Sweet Lord', and said it wasn't 'He's So Fine' he'd ripped off, but 'Oh Happy Day.' George lost his case, but incredibly, my friend won.

A few months after arriving in London I ran into a guy I knew from school busking at Notting Hill Gate tube. We started talking about how you could always tell where the best pitches were as there'd be a 'Buskers Will Be Prosecuted' sign opposite. I then noticed the one opposite him was only hanging on by a couple of screws and decided to take it for my own wall. I managed to prize it off and was walking up the stairs with it under my arm when an off-duty cop who'd been watching the whole thing told me I was under arrest.

I was given a duty solicitor who said if I pleaded guilty, I'd most likely just get a small fine, though it also meant I'd have a criminal record saying I'd been done for theft (it doesn't specify what you stole), meaning a lifetime of potential employment issues and possibly never being able to play or even visit the US.

I felt like I'd fucked up everything when about a week before the hearing I remembered something from my A Level law studies. For a successful criminal conviction under UK law, two things must be established: that you did something illegal (actus reus, meaning "guilty act") and that you intended to do it (mens rea, or guilty mind). The latter is to prevent someone being prosecuted for accidentally picking up someone else's bag, for example. The mens rea for theft is defined as "the intention to permanently deprive."

I went back to my lawyer and told him there was something I'd forgotten to mention and that when I'd originally taken the sign it was as a kind of practical joke, so if the Transport Police tried to arrest my friend for busking, he could say he didn't realise it was forbidden as there was no sign to say so. (Hilarious, huh?) Had I not been caught, I told him I would have left the sign outside the station, where I felt sure it would be found by someone from London Transport and returned to its rightful place. The point being that I wasn't intending to permanently deprive LT of their sign, only to deprive them *temporarily*.

My lawyer gave me a sly look and said it was worth a try. He then spoke with their lawyer who offered to drop the charge if I agreed to being 'bound over' for twelve months, in other words, no fine or criminal record as long as I wasn't convicted of anything else in that time. I accepted and have somehow maintained a clean record to this day.

A French musician I know used a lateral approach to get out of National Service (which they still have over there). Almost everyone tries to avoid it, so it's impressive he succeeded.

There was an initial interview where they asked about his social life and what he did for a living. He said he didn't have any friends and made his money selling drugs. He was then sent for his medical. He'd made sure not to shower or change his clothing for the previous two weeks. The room was also very small. His impression of the examiner's face when he dropped his trousers was priceless.

WHO WRITES THE SONGS?

Tues 10 Oct 2006

Songwriting is a funny thing. I can go a couple of months and produce nothing but a few scraps of lyrics and some dirgey bits of melody. Then all of a sudden a mood descends and a rush of ideas come so thick and fast, it's a struggle to get them all down. There's usually some fine-tuning and polishing to do, but it can be surprisingly minimal - I've had songs fully complete in half an hour. When I come back to it, I sometimes notice little melodic themes, internal rhymes and other bits of "cleverness" I didn't consciously intend, and I'm left wondering how I managed it in such a short time. It seems like something I spent days or weeks crafting and sweating over. Usually they sound better than the ones I have spent weeks sweating over.

Sometimes I've had the bulk of the song come in one go, but got stuck. There might be a lyric I don't like or it needs another part. I can come up with lots of ideas that more or less do the job, but none feel like the "right" one somehow. Then maybe months later a line or melody comes into my head and it's "Eureka!" I know instantly it's what I was looking for (not that I really knew what I was looking for), and when I add it, not only does it fit perfectly with the bits before and after, but it adds just the right amount of weight, humour or whatever the song felt like it was lacking and prevented me from letting it go.

When stuff like this happens, rather than being the composer, it feels like my role was closer to that of a secretary taking down ideas (perhaps down a dodgy phoneline?), then being left the job of putting it all together.

I'm not the first musician to have these thoughts. Keith Richards compared the process to an aerial receiving signals from the ether; Hendrix compared it to automatic writing; Neil Young to "fishing," and numerous others have talked of songs coming to them complete or feeling like they were acting as some kind of conduit. It would be easier to dismiss if not for the quality of some of the material it's been claimed for. Pete Townsend said most of The Who's rock opera *Tommy* was "received." John Lennon said 'Nowhere Man' came to him in one go ("words, music, the whole damn thing") as did 'Across the Universe' - a song that even mentions words floating through the air. Similar statements have come from classical composers as well as poets, authors and artists.

Yet even as I write this I feel uneasy - and not just for putting my name next to those of people like Hendrix and Pete Townshend. Because there's something about the idea of 'divine' inspiration or whatever one calls it that goes against the fundamentally throwaway spirit on which rock 'n' roll was founded and some of the best of it was made. Was Iggy Pop really connecting to some higher plane when he sang 'I Wanna Be Your Dog'? Or the Sex Pistols when they wrote 'Anarchy in the UK'?

There's another reason I feel uncomfortable, as even talking about this topic, I'm breaking an artistic superstition that says one should never analyse the source of one's creativity as to do so can endanger it, inviting that most-feared condition of creative impotence known as "losing it."

I doubt I need to offer examples. The list of artists who went from genius to near irrelevance sometimes in a few short years is as long as it is depressing, and nowhere is the phenomenon more common than rock music.

Which creates a paradox. Because the fact there's so clearly this 'it' that can be lost suggests something mysterious about creativity, marking it out from simple craftsmanship (did you ever hear of a carpenter suddenly losing his ability to build a wall cabinet?), and yet we're supposed not to think about it, even if it's to seek a solution. So I should probably stop this now.

Yeah, right. Like that's going to happen.

Perhaps the most dramatic case of 'losing it' is that of Brian Wilson, the tortured genius behind most of the Beach Boys' biggest hits including 'Surfin' Safari', 'Fun, Fun, Fun', 'California Girls' and what's considered their crowning glory, the *Pet Sounds* album. Featuring majestic, semi-orchestrated arrangements and themes of innocence and loss, it was a radical departure from the mainly three-chord songs about surfing, cars and girls that made them the biggest US band of the time. Even the seasoned session pro's Brian brought in to work on it were amazed by the 23-year-old's production and songwriting skills, and it was immediately hailed a masterpiece by the pop aristocracy of the time including members of The Beatles, Stones and The Who, while their label Capitol began printing up badges proclaiming "the God-like genius of Brian Wilson."

Despite the acclaim, the album only just made the Billboard Top 50, to the irritation of some in the band who'd warned Brian against the change in direction (on first hearing the backing tracks, Mike Love famously accused him of "fucking with the formula"). But Brian was always more concerned with creative success, however, and set to work on what he promised would trump even *Pet Sounds* - the soon-to-be notorious *Smile* LP.

It got off to a great start. Brian debuted a solo version of 'Surf's Up' (intended for the album) on a show hosted by conductor Leonard Bernstein, where it was compared to that of serious classical works. But as the sessions dragged on, he seemed to lose direction, endlessly re-working parts and becoming racked by indecision.

With a mounting studio bill and little to show for it, the more conservative elements within the band persuaded Capitol that Brian had finally "gone too far" and conspired to release *Smiley Smile*, a mish-mash of semi-completed *Smile* tracks and re-recordings with only minimal input from their composer.

Brian had already been acting strangely, but he now seems to enter full-blown psychosis. He would spend the next thirty years battling terrifying inner demons, with tales of him wandering around Hollywood barefoot, hiding in cupboards and at one point applying for a job in a health store. Brian had suffered a breakdown prior to this, but while the first led them to spending his time in the studio and a blossoming of his creativity, the second all but killed it.

Though he made some recordings during this time, by his own admission they never matched his earlier works, in particular *Pet Sounds* which he still refers to as "holy music." (Brian was a strong believer in the notion of 'artist as conduit', sometimes starting sessions with prayers for divine assistance.)

In an effort to reconnect to his Muse, Brian tried various diets, gurus and therapies. He seems to have made some recovery of late, mentally and creatively, and with the help of some younger musicians had even managed to complete his own version of *Smile*. He recently said it was his failure to deliver the promised masterpiece that led to his problems, but what caused him to lose his musical way in the first place?

Some blame this simply on his (prodigious) drug intake. Others say the trigger was *Sgt. Pepper* which came out while working on *Smile* and which he supposedly felt he could never top (Brian felt a strong artistic rivalry with The Beatles). He was also dealing with various personal stresses, including the breakdown of his marriage and a pending lawsuit over songwriting royalties.

The product of an abusive household (the deafness in his right ear is thought to have resulted from an early beating from his father, Murray), Brian had always been a fragile soul. One day Murray bought a piano for the house. As soon as he began pounding the keys, Brian found he could screen out the abuse around and actually feel happy for a change.

As his playing improved, he persuaded his brothers Carl and Dennis plus cousin Mike Love to form a group. Ever the opportunist, Murray appointed himself manager, secured them a small deal, and within a few months they had their first hit.

Like most musicians, it seems Brian's primary motivation was to play the stuff he liked and have a bit of fun (fun, fun). Photos from the *Pet Sounds* sessions show how much he and the other musicians were enjoying themselves. By the time of *Smile* (ironically), the expressions are mostly drawn and tense. With the lawsuit hanging over him and both Capitol and the other Beach Boys breathing down his neck, the music that had been a refuge from his problems was now the source of them, the studio once his playground was now a battlefield. In short, the fun had gone.

I believe all great art comes from a spirit of fun and playfulness, and once that's left the process, it's usually not long before the quality follows. Having "fun" doesn't mean you have to be grinning from ear to ear the whole time, nor does the subject matter have to be happy. It's more a matter of being completely absorbed by what you're working on, and it could be a story of a twisted childkiller as long as it's fascinating to the author. Not all of the process is likely to be enjoyable. There can be a lot of hard work involved, especially in the later fine-tuning stage, but if it's not enjoyable at least at the conception, it's unlikely to have a deep impact on an audience.

This is relatively easy when starting out and your only ambition is to play a few parties and/or impress some girls. But should success result, following your artistic whims can start to look like an indulgence, in the knowledge that one flop is often all it takes to finish a career. And it's not just your livelihood that depends on you continuing to come up with the commercial goods, but also that of your bandmates, management, etc., all of whom will have their own idea of what direction you should be going and how much you can afford to "fuck with the formula." And that's not even mentioning pressures from the record label. Maybe this is why "losing it" is so common among rock musicians.

So was the "it" that Brian and so many others lost merely the enjoyment? And where does this leave the notion of the "artist as conduit"?

A few years ago I was given a book on mediumship issued by the College of Psychic Studies and was struck by the similarity of the initial creative state and what it said was the optimum for receiving psychic impressions (relaxed, but alert – passively noting all impressions regardless of whether they appear to make logical sense). It also advised against forcing results (John Lennon said 'Nowhere Man' came to him when he went to lie down after spending five hours trying to come up with "something meaningful") and not to worry if nothing came, maintaining a kind of "so what?" indifference both to failure and success, focussing only on the job in hand.

This indifference to success seems common to many great artists - at least while they were being great - and can almost be seen as an indicator of creative good health. Prior to *Tommy*, Pete Townsend described The Who's entire output as "rubbish." The Beatles were also dismissive of their previous works including *Sgt. Pepper*. Others with long careers such as Bowie, Dylan, Neil Young and Nick Cave have also often burned their musical bridges by refusing to play old material or periodically reinventing themselves.

For most of the '60s Brian Wilson also seemed focussed only on his current work. Like many acts then, he was working so hard - producing up to four albums a year – it gave little opportunity to dwell on past successes.

But at some point during the protracted *Smile* sessions, I believe he took a step back to ponder his previous creation. Realising what he'd achieved through fun, hard work and whatever strange magic helped inspire it, he became as in awe as others. With all the accolades flying, he began to wonder if he could repeat the trick, let alone surpass it as he'd been boasting.

Just as a mountaineer shouldn't look down lest he lose his nerve, an artist shouldn't look back. The more he worried, the further removed he became from the creative source, until a paralysis began to set in. Any hope of regaining his confidence was then destroyed by having the album taken off him - and he's been in mourning for his lost Muse ever since.

Ultimately, it was the success of *Pet Sounds* that led to the failure of *Smile* and his subsequent problems. If he wants to fully regain his powers, I believe he needs to step from its shadow - perhaps denounce it as the saccharine whimsy that harsher critics have accused it of and return to making music for its own sake. Should the Muse bestow her blessings, brilliant; if not, at least he'll have enjoyed himself.

To those of a more scientific bent, the whole notion of divine inspiration is probably nonsense anyway and can be attributed simply to the latent, incredible powers of the human brain. They might also point out that creativity is mainly an occupation of the right hemisphere, which would explain why left brain activity such as self-doubt, worry or even analysing the subject would tend to inhibit it.

The two viewpoints are not necessarily incompatible. Inspiration could still involve a mediumistic element, while requiring a certain frame of mind to enter it.

A more compelling counter-argument, in my view, is the fact that most great works are easily recognisable as being written by their composer. You wouldn't confuse a Bob Dylan song with one by Brian, for example, which shouldn't be the case if they're all drawing from the same source. Rather than being something external, this might suggest "the God is within" (as many mystics have claimed) or a more dualistic 'God is my co-writer' type thing.

Personally, I can accept that a song like 'Never Gonna Give You Up' can be written through craft alone, but to produce something as musically "out-there" and lyrically profound as 'Across the Universe' in one short sitting is a lot less convincing.

But in the end, it doesn't really matter, as one's approach should be the same either way. I also find it reassuring that if there is some kind of God involved, it seems he wants us to be happy.

THE TEACHERS WHO TAUGHT ME WEREN'T COOL

Wed 11 0ct 2006

One of my brothers recently went to some reunion at Holmewood House, the prep school all the boys in our family attended. At one point a former Housemaster pointed to a covered portrait of who he said was the school's most famous ex-pupil. He pulled it back to reveal a giant blow-up of Shane McGowan of the Pogues in all his toothless, grinning glory. (Yes, he really did go to private school.)

Holmewood was pretty strict, though probably typical of most prep schools back then - standing up when teachers entered the room, calling them "sir" and all of that, but it had a good academic record and a charismatic and well-liked Headmaster called Mr Bairamian. He had a way of making you feel both proud to be a member of the school and valued.

His assemblies were full of inspiring stories and rousing speeches. If any of the school teams had won a match, he'd bound around the stage re-enacting the highlights as if it was the most exciting sporting event since England last took the Ashes. It turned out the school's record was at least partly due to him 'assisting' various boys with their exam papers. When this came out, he was quietly moved to a lesser known school that either didn't know or didn't care.

His replacement was Mr Liversedge. He wasn't a bad person, just dull and humourless, especially compared to his predecessor.

Assemblies soon became dreary affairs where he'd be droning on about how we all just needed to pull our socks up or complaining about some minor issue (crisp wrappers in the urinals seemed to be an obsession).

How easy a time you had at the school depended a lot on which House you were put in or, more specifically, its Housemaster. Unfortunately, mine was Mr Burdon, a chain-smoking, heavy-drinking ogre of a man with a reputation for physical violence. I once saw him come up behind a boy of 8, who hadn't seen him enter the room and was still talking to his friend in assembly, then belted him across the back of his head with the full force of his bloated frame. I think he had some kind of warning about this, as at some point the hitting stopped, but his verbal assaults were almost as frightening. He'd regularly haul someone in front of the House for a vicious dressing-down, sometimes reducing them to tears.

The only lessons I enjoyed were English and art, so there wasn't a lot to look forward to, but the worst part of the day for me were often lunchtimes, as it was compulsory to eat everything we were served and which on a bad day really was sub-prison slop.

It was soon my routine each morning break I'd go straight to the area outside the kitchens and try to sniff out what was being prepared. If it was something bearable like spaghetti or beefburgers, I'd relax and go to play 'ball-he' or whatever was the latest playground craze. But every few days I'd be greeted by some foul-smelling gristle-filled stew or my personal nightmare - fish pie packed with lumpy bits of egg and a liberal scattering of bones, and I'd then spend the next two periods in a state of dread at the ordeal to come.

After that it was mainly a case of damage limitation, starting by pleading with the cooks to give you as small a portion as possible. You'd then take that to the dining room, hoping one of the more liberal teachers would be on your table like Mr Dear, the Art Head, or Mrs Christie who taught French. They'd usually let you off the worst of it as long as you made a valiant attempt at the vegetables or more edible stuff. If you were unlucky, it would be Burdon or one of the other sadists like Mr Souter, another maths/sports teacher, or Mr Hunter, the permanently sneering history teacher.

You could sometimes get away with flicking a few bits off your plate onto the floor, which you'd then either tread in or kick towards someone else. I once saw someone tip his into his blazer pockets to deposit outside later Colditz style. There were always a few kids who'd eat anything, so the most common method was to pick away slowly at whatever you could manage (if necessary while holding your nose accompanied by glugs of water) until a few of them had finished. You were allowed to leave obviously inedible stuff like bones and fat, so eventually there'd be a pile of plates in the centre with their collective leftovers on top. Then as soon as whoever was supervising wasn't looking or left the table to refill the water jug, you'd scrape everything you had onto the top plate, slide yours to the bottom and then put on the most innocent expression you could. It was risky, though.

Once we'd been served some experimental green curry not even the iron-stomached lot could handle, and a boy was caught scraping his leftovers onto this huge pile by the head of the first year Mrs Gledhill, who then made him eat the lot.

After lunch came sport which I also hated, at least the winter ones which we had to play almost regardless of the weather. How people can enjoy chasing a ball in the driving rain for an hour and a half is something I still don't get. No namby-pamby underwear allowed either - plus occasional on-pitch checks and the humiliation of having to remove them in front of everyone if caught. Utter fucking misery as far as I was concerned.

At the start of my third year my heart sank when I saw I'd been put into Burdon's maths class. Not long after arriving at the school he'd come up to tell me my eldest brother was the cleverest pupil he'd ever taught and that he expected great things of me. Perhaps because I'd failed so spectacularly to meet his expectations, his attitude towards me seemed to gradually harden, until I felt certain he'd pencilled me in for one of his verbal assaults.

I'd never really given him a real opportunity, though, until a couple of weeks into that term. Having given us the basics of simultaneous equations, he told us to start answering questions from our textbooks three at a time and then bring them up for marking.

Somehow I'd got ahead of everyone when I came to an equation that didn't seem to resolve. Unsure what to do, I ended up writing, "These equations are not simultaneous," then nervously went up to his desk. He ticked two of the answers, then put down his pen, let out an exaggerated loud sigh. He told the class to stop what they were doing and turn to the question I couldn't make work.

"Would you like to know what Briffa's given as his answer? He's written, 'These equations are not simultaneous.' *(Pause for dramatic effect.)* 'These...equations...are not...simultaneous.'"

I heard a couple of groans.

He then turned to me, "Do you know what you are, Briffa?"

"No, sir."

"Then I'll tell you. You're a silly... ignorant.... childish... immature...f eeble...juvenile..." with each insult his voice grew louder and his face redder.

Just as he looked ready to go fully ballistic, I saw him glance at his textbook, presumably thinking he should double-check, and saw I was correct. His expression then turned to an even uglier forced smile as he tried desperately to back pedal.

"...Oh, no you're not!... Oh, no you're not!... You're actually a very ...clever...boy...though what you should *really* have written was…" (followed by a load of maths jargon no 11-year-old could possibly have known).

It should have been one of those punch-the-air moments. Instead, I became even more worried, as I knew he'd be absolutely determined to get me now.

He soon got his moment. A week or two later I gave another leftfield answer in a test he'd set us. I could have justified it had I been given the chance, but he wasn't going to make that mistake. By the time he'd finished, he'd ripped into everything from my personality to my physical appearance and loud enough (as I would discover) to halt classes in the whole block.

For the next few days I was a virtual pariah, and I ended up so terrified of the guy, I started feigning illnesses just to avoid his classes. I missed around half the term as a result. Fortunately, it was the only one I had him for.

I'd also been having issues with a Latin teacher, not because he hated me, though - quite the reverse. Mr Quick was what he called "a bit of a bender" with a penchant for pre-pubescents. To my knowledge he never directly interfered with anyone, but there were various stories circulating about him walking in while boys were showering or suggesting skinny dips on nature walks. His main kink was spanking, which he'd usually arrange by picking myself or one of the other boys he had a thing for and asking some grammar question. If you got it wrong, he'd tell you to "swat up" on whatever it was and then come to his room after lunch for testing. He'd usually have the lights lowered and in a huskier voice than normal would tell you to go through whatever you were meant to have learned, until you made a mistake. He'd then give you a light spank over his knee and tell you to continue.

I probably had this four or five times. Once he told me to pull down my trousers, then spanked me over my underpants, but that was the furthest it went. Afterwards he'd look guilty and usually say something like, "You won't tell your parents, will you?"

As strange as this may sound, more than anything I felt sorry for him. He was a decent guy in all other respects (and a very good teacher), and I could see he lived in constant fear that any one of us might bring his life crashing down at any moment. If he'd gone any further, I'm sure I'd feel very different, but I'd be lying if I said it was any more than an inconvenience and a bit embarrassing, and I still don't bear him serious malice.

He actually was found out in the end. Someone in my class decided to write down the various rumours in a little book and was showing it around when a teacher walked in and confiscated it. A few days later he was asked if the stories were true, and a couple of weeks after that Quick stopped coming in to school. I remember an announcement one assembly that he wouldn't be coming for a while due to "back problems" and a friend whispering to me, "Back problems, my arse – my dad's seen him working behind the bar in his local pub."

To prepare us for the full-time boarding schools most of us were going on to, you were expected (at least) to weekly board for your final term. My main concern about this were the twice-weekly communal bath sessions which were sometimes supervised by a Swedish matron most of us fancied called Kirsten. I was just hitting adolescence and springing erections at the mildest of stimuli. The prospect of getting a hard-on while sitting opposite another naked boy was real and terrifying - the sort of thing you didn't come back from.

Boarding also meant more time around Burden, who continued to be a complete bastard. He came into our dorm one night brandishing a cricket bat and threatening to bring it down on the legs of anyone he caught talking.

Talking of cricket, that was one sport I enjoyed. I was never good enough to make any of the school teams, though, until one Saturday I got a call at home asking if I was free to play for the First 11 at the next day's match against another Holmewood at their grounds in Essex. It was one of the big fixtures of the season, and because of the name thing there was a lot of rivalry involved.

They batted first and scored a much higher total than we were expecting and then proceeded to quickly bowl out most of our best players until it was obvious we couldn't win, but could still achieve a (respectable) draw as long as they didn't bowl the whole team out before the allotted overs.

We were down to our final two players plus me in reserve (I was number eleven, naturally) when on the first ball of the final over disaster struck as one of them was bowled out. Our captain came to give me a quick pep talk, reminding me I had just five balls to survive and to play as safely as possible and not worry about scoring any runs.

The first two balls were wide enough I was able to leave them, but the next was straight. I moved into a standard 'blocking' position. Had I been using my usual cheapo plank of wood bat, this would almost certainly have driven the ball safely into the ground. However, just before going in, someone had offered to lend me their notoriously springy Gray-Nicolls' dug-out. The ball bounced off it about twenty feet into the air and into the bowler's hands. I couldn't have made it easier if I'd been giving catching practise. That was a lo-oong journey home.

At the end of the year, each House held a leavers party that included a little ceremony where they'd give out prefect ties to anyone who'd yet to be made one. I was one of these, which was very unusual as I'd passed my common entrance exam by this point and been awarded an art scholarship, both of which carried a tie as automatic.

With only a few days left of term, the whole thing was an empty gesture, but I was looking forward to receiving mine, as I'd decided to refuse it. I was no longer scared of Burdon, and I wanted him to know what I thought of him. Unfortunately, I never got the chance and was the only person in the school to leave without one. He clearly hated me to the end.

Burdon then made a speech saying if he'd sometimes been tough on us, it was only because he cared so much, and then finished by saying if any of us were passing his place in the future to be sure to drop by to say hi. "...And if I'm not in, the back door's always open, so just grab a beer from the fridge and make yourself at home until I get in."

My brother who went to the reunion told me he made the same speech when he left, and we once speculated what would happen if someone ever took up his offer and Burdon walked in to find some stranger in his living room drinking his beer. Come at them with a cricket bat, I reckoned.

(A few months after writing this, I saw an article saying Mr Quick had been given a six-month prison sentence for indecency. In the comments section a few former pupils posted also expressing a degree of sympathy and saying they liked him otherwise.)

IF YOU WANT TO GET ON, GET A HAT

Thurs 12 Oct 2006

Toby, the Hatcham Social guy, moved in a couple of days ago, and last night we went to the Notting Hill Arts Club together. He'd been wearing a trilby, but about an hour after we got there, he came over to say he'd lost it. I wandered around to see if anyone had it on, but without any luck.

Quite a few people seemed to be in hats, though, including a guy in a big cowboy number. I'd been observing him earlier on account of the fact that cowboy hats are part of a pulling technique Neil Strauss talks about in *The Game* called "peacocking." Anything eye-catching will do. He also suggests platform heels or those flashing necklaces - the idea being to stand out from the crowd and look generally alpha male-ish. I've noticed a lot of guys doing stuff that looks like it's come from *The Game* lately. This combined with how he'd been leering at just about every girl that passed, made me think this was why he was wearing his.

If so, it wasn't doing him much good. He'd ended up alone on the dancefloor looking awkward in his big hat, and now he was at the bar still on his own and looking self-conscious - as if wishing he'd never come out in the thing.

I was almost feeling sorry for him when a blonde girl sidled up next to where he was standing. She gave him a couple of sideways glances, then flicked the brim of the hat and said something I couldn't hear, but would bet money was, "Hey, cowboy!"

About twenty minutes later he was back on the dancefloor with the blonde rubbing against him and another brunette close to them both - my "having a babe on your arm is like a great reference on your CV" theory in action.

Even though I understand why these techniques work, seeing all this played out in front of me made me feel suddenly depressed. Was that really all it took to make a girl think you have it going on - a £20 cowboy hat? Maybe if he'd been a bit cooler, but from what I'd seen he wasn't even good at the Game. To be honest, the blonde wasn't that hot, but the brunette was definitely cute. If he pulled her, it would be definitely messing with the natural order or - God forbid - both of them. So while I don't normally agree with muscling in on another guy's territory, in this case I felt a moral duty. Nothing whatsoever to do with jealousy.

There's apparently this thing that's big on the online "PUA" (pick-up artist) scene called "field reports." This is where guys post accounts of their previous night's pulling attempts for others to either learn from or critique, depending on their success.

So I'm going to make this my own field report, using the "Instinctive Approach" that I discussed in the 'How to Pick Up Girls Pt. 2' essay. This is where you say and do whatever comes into your head while trying to stay as alert and in the moment as you can. Like a jazz player improvising a solo, if you're lucky, you can surprise yourself at what comes out and how you can break the accepted rules. PUAs usually use an alias. Neil Strauss calls himself "Style," so I'm going with "Scruff."

A REPORT FROM FIELD the night of 11/10/06 by Scruff.

The two girls were now standing with the guy in the bar area. At some point he went to the gent's, which I took as my cue to move in. The brunette had her back to me, so I tapped her on the shoulder.

"Excuse me, have you heard of a book called *The Game*?"
"I'm sorry?"
"*The Game*. Have you heard of it?"
"Er, no."
"Oh, okay, then."

A few seconds later she came back, "I did once see a film called *The Game*."

"Really? What was it about?"

She gave a brief description.

"No, it's not that."

"...So what's this book about?"

"It's about picking up women, as in seducing them."

"Ri-iiight. And so why would I want to read a book like that?"

"Because a lot of guys have been reading it lately, and you might want to know some of the methods in case someone tries one on you - 'know your enemy.'"

"Actually, I think I have heard of that. It has things like, 'If you fancy a girl, go up to her friend first.'"

"That's it – although that's quite a basic one."

"Well, they wouldn't work. Not on me anyway."

"Let me guess. Because you're far too clever to fall for some kind of set routine or technique?"

She gave me a really dirty look, "Well, yes – as a matter of fact!"
"I don't think so."

"Oh, really? And why's that?"

"Because you're already falling for one."

"So you're using a technique?"

"Yes and no."

"...All right, then. Show me another."

"Okay. Think of a number between 1 and 10."

"...Got one."

"7."

She looked taken aback. "How did you know that?"

"I can read minds." (That one is actually taken directly from *The Game*. For some reason, people almost always choose 7.)

"Try another."

"Maybe later. The point is, it works. You're intrigued."

"You haven't seduced me, though."

"But you're still talking to me - one step at a time. Anyway, I don't believe in techniques. I think they're immoral."

"So why did you read this book?"

"Because I wrote a play about pulling women and someone who saw it said I should read *The Game* as it had some similar ideas."

"You wrote a play about pulling women?"

"Yes, but that doesn't mean I'd use those techniques myself. As I said, I think they're wrong."

She looked confused. "So what else does *The Game* recommend?"

"Wearing a cowboy hat."

"I hate cowboy hats."

"Really? So why were you just talking to someone in one?"

"He's a friend."

I have to admit this threw me. I still reckoned he'd worn it to "peacock," but it was a reminder I didn't have the whole situation sussed and should probably tone down the smart-guy stuff.

I asked her name (Maria), and we then got into a less adversarial conversation about *The Rules* (a kind of female version of *The Game*) and self-help books in general, including the one that supposedly started the trend - *How to Win Friends and Influence People*. I said I'd read an article about it recently by someone who wanted to see if the advice still held. One of its points was that you make more friends losing an argument than by winning it, as winning just makes them feel bad about themselves. I said that women seemed to understand this better than guys.

"Absolutely. Men are idiots!" she said. "That's why I don't bother with *The Rules* - I don't need them. I could have any guy here if I wanted."

"I'm sure you could. But only for sex, not a relationship. And that's not what you're really looking for, are you?"

"What do you mean? I love sex."

"Sure, but not with a complete stranger - unless you really fancied him. You'd rather it was with someone you were in love with, right? Or at least knew a bit? Go on a couple of dates first?...which is when you start having to do the work and playing the games. Whereas I may struggle to get laid, I can get a date any time I want."

I offered to prove it by getting her to pick out any girl she wanted and seeing if I could get her to agree to go for dinner. She was up for it, but then we got side-tracked and started talking about something unrelated.

A bit later, she suddenly turned her back on me and began talking to some people she knew. It felt like she wanted to make a point rather than wanting to end the conversation. I gave it a couple of minutes and then tapped her on the shoulder.

"How are you doing?"

She'd obviously been mulling over our conversation as she suddenly went into one.

"The thing is, you make out like girls are exactly the same and want the same things, but we're actually, you know...different?"

"Of course. Still there are some things virtually none of you want."

"So what is it that none of us want, Mr Expert *(ouch)*?"

"Some loser arsehole, like all the others out there. *(I gestured to the crowd.)* You want someone who's not just like everyone else. Someone a little bit...special. Right?"

She didn't say anything.

"...which is why the mind-reading thing works. And the cowboy hat."

"Hmmm."

We'd been talking for at least an hour by this point, and despite the verbal sparring, I think she'd enjoyed it or she wouldn't have stuck around. But as far as pulling, I knew I'd blown it, ironically, by making the exact mistake warned against in *How To Win Friends...* and made it seem like I knew more about women than she did. And if she left with me now, it would just make her look like this complete ditz who'd been played from start to finish.

Despite a strong opening, Scruff's ego got in the way, and the solo slipped into self-indulgence.

I offered her a drink, but just as we got to the bar, it shut (further evidence I'd fallen out with the Tao). A few minutes later the lights came up, and I left without asking for her number - no point risking that humiliation.

Outside I saw Toby. He'd also had an interesting night. Having arrived with enough money for a single beer, he put it down after one swig, and it somehow broke in his hand. Later some girl blew him out, who it turned out was the one who originally took his trilby, but he got it back at least.

To be honest, I doubt I'd have pulled Maria whatever I'd said (she was quite a bit younger). Even if I had, I doubt I'd have been much use. It didn't occur to me when I started these essays that it would mean going 30 days without a full day off. I'm also having to do some editing and rewriting as I go along, and I'm beginning to feel pretty knackered from it all.

MY LIFE WITH THE BEATLES

Fri 13 Oct 2006

BAD BOY
You may have noticed I mention The Beatles quite a lot. If you didn't get it, the title of the other day's essay on Holmewood ('The Teachers Who Taught Me Weren't Cool') was a line from 'Getting Better.' It was actually Holmewood where I discovered them. I was passing the assembly hall one lunchbreak with a friend called Goddard ("God" as we called him) when we saw they were rehearsing some end-of-year review show and decided to check it out.

The final "sketch" had the parents of two kids telling them they were going away for the weekend and to be sure to behave themselves while they were gone. As soon as they walked off, the kids put The Beatles' version of 'Bad Boy' on the stereo and the rest of the cast came back on for a big party/dance finale.

The house I grew up in had one of those little Dansette record players and just four LPs - Vince Hill's *Greatest Hits* being about the most cutting edge. So this was the first time I'd heard a proper rock 'n' roll song at any real volume, and it was like I'd been plugged into the mains. I had goose pimples and shivers; I'd never experienced anything so uplifting. Two and half minutes later in a state of religious-like ecstasy/shock I asked God if he happened to know who the song was by. Not only did he know, but he owned a copy - or at least his mum did. I asked if there was any way I could come over to hear it again. He lived a few miles from me, but he ended up arranging for me to stay the following weekend.

Along with *Oldies But Goldies* (the compilation 'Bad Boy' came from) the Goddards also owned *With The Beatles*, *A Hard Day's Night* and *Revolver*, plus a proper stereo - a revelation in itself.

I was soon staying over as often as I could, and through their music God and I became best friends. Songs like 'Devil in Her Heart,' and 'I'm Happy Just to Dance With You' formed the perfect soundtrack to our endless discussions about the girls we fancied and how we planned to win them. Of the four albums, *Revolver* was the most intriguing. I couldn't even work out what some of the instruments were - even their voices sounded strange. God told me they'd been "on drugs" while making it, something I'd always considered dangerous and sleazy. Now I wasn't so sure.

There was only so much his family could take of me playing the same four records more or less on repeat. They had some other interesting stuff like Elvis and the Stones, but The Beatles always seemed to hold an extra magic, and I was also becoming curious about their other albums. It was time to buy my first record.

As my birthday was approaching, I asked my mum for some German greatest hits collection (the only Beatles record our local shop had in stock). By the time I'd rendered that near unplayable, it was coming up to Christmas, so I got her to order their first album *Please Please Me*, while my brother and I managed to talk my dad into buying a Winthronics music centre as a present for the house.

For the next couple of months, as soon as I came in from school I'd run straight to our living room, put on the headphones and play both sides straight through, and if I didn't have too much homework, both sides again. Instantly I'd be transported to a realm of chiming guitars and aching harmonies sung by people who knew the agony of unrequited love that I was currently experiencing, but could somehow turn it into the most joyous sound ever. "There's a place, where I can go..."

I still love that album. Some consider it a bit throwaway, but if you can get past the light subject matter, it's packed with soul and drenched in atmosphere. I was delighted when years later I discovered John rated it as one their top three.

I started saving my pocket money, and a couple of months later bought *Beatles For Sale* via mail order, followed by a second-hand copy of *Rubber Soul* - quickly becoming my new favourite. At some point a friend passed on some Italian two-EP set containing six songs from *Sgt. Pepper*. If *Revolver* was a bit out there, this sounded like it was beamed from another planet.

While I'd believed we only had four LPs in our house, it turned out this wasn't quite the case. One day an image came into my head of a white, square, flat object I vaguely remembered gathering dust on a shelf in my eldest brother's room. I ran up, and sure enough, sitting there the whole time was a copy of the White Album bought during his brief hippy phase. It was especially fortunate being their one double and therefore most expensive. I'd got used to their albums sounding very different from one another, but it was the first time they sounded unhappy to me. At times the atmosphere bordered on sinister. Still brilliant, of course.

A few weeks later I was sent to boarding school - a miserable experience where music was one of the only pleasures. Through some judicious buying and selling, I added *Help* and *Magical Mystery Tour* to my collection, along with other stuff like The Yardbirds, Dylan and The Kinks.

During the first set of holidays I hooked up with God, but something had changed. He was now listening to Ritchie Blackmore's Rainbow, who he actually claimed were as good as The Beatles. Luckily, I'd found a new Beatle buddy, Anthony 'Harold' Wilson. Like me, he was learning guitar and didn't seem to mind accompanying me on the songs I'd been writing since first hearing 'Bad Boy'.

Harold also had a radio, and every Sunday we'd tune in to the Old Record Club and add names like The Yardbirds and The

Lovin' Spoonful to our list of artists to explore. A big problem prior to the internet and CD reissues was simply finding a copy of whatever you wanted to buy. You could go to great lengths just to listen to something you'd heard good reports of. I remember spending a whole lunch break with my ear pressed to a door where someone was playing *Live at the Hollywood Bowl* - a muffled recording at the best of times.

As I added *Magical Mystery Tour* and the full-length *Sgt. Pepper* to my collection, buying Beatles records was becoming an increasingly bittersweet experience, aware that with each purchase I was getting closer to when there'd be no more new Beatle music to hear.

That day has long since passed, but while I probably haven't heard a proper new Beatles song since I was 16, they continue to bring enormous pleasure. Numerous times I've found myself standing under some crappy speaker in a bar or shop when their music came on unexpectedly, transfixed by some unusual percussion part or wandering bass line I'd somehow never fully appreciated before and couldn't leave until the last note had faded.

BEATLEMANIAX

Reading this, you may have been reminded of someone similarly obsessed you went to school or maybe once worked with. I'm not just talking about your regular fan who owns four or five albums and thinks they were a great band. I'm talking about the out-and-out fanatic who owns every single album, some solo records, maybe some bootlegs and items of memorabilia and to whom they weren't just a great band, but by far and away the greatest of all time. Give them the opportunity and they'll tell their own story of the record that got them hooked, the friends they made as a result and how as much as they love other music, no one else seems to do it for them on quite the same level.

All major artists have their fanatics, but there's a level of obsession with The Beatles you rarely see among fans of acts like The Stones or Led Zep, and evidenced by the books they seem to constantly devour. Of the 2,000-plus so far published, it's not uncommon for a serious fan to have read 20 or 30. One friend and fellow obsessive has two shelves devoted solely to them. Stones or Led Zep fans might own every album and adorn their walls with their posters, but they rarely read 30 books on them. I'm not sure there's been that many written on the latter.

Along with this obsession, The Beatles seem to inspire a unique form of contempt. To some, the mere mention of their name risks a torrent of abuse and vitriolic attacks on everything from their image to Ringo's drumming to individual songs (expect 'Maxwell's Silver Hammer' and 'The Frog Chorus' to get a mention). If pushed, they may concede to liking a couple of their songs, usually - though not necessarily – written by John, who they'll probably admit some respect for, though of course it was George Martin they really owed their success to.

I've noticed it's fans of the aforementioned major acts, The Stones, Led Zep, etc., who are most likely to come out with this stuff, which I don't think is a coincidence. Rather than hating them, I suspect it's more that they consider them (vastly) overrated and hearing them constantly referred to as 'The Greatest Band of All Time' (t.m.) above whoever they think deserves that title is bound to stick in the craw eventually. There also seems to be a confusion, because they genuinely don't get why so many people are in awe of what to them is a slightly above-average pop band or why they haven't gone the way of people like The Hollies or Cliff Richard, also huge in their day, but increasingly irrelevant with each passing year. Instead of diminishing their status, time has consolidated it, making their achievements appear even more extraordinary as they continue to outsell any existing band decades after their split (the recent *1* collection was the fastest selling album of all time).

For the benefit of such people, I thought I'd use this

opportunity to try and explain the fascination and why even if you can't stand their music, you should still be amazed by them. Plus I'll take any excuse to talk about them. So if you are willing, try to forget the suits and 'Maxwell's Silver Hammer' for a moment and imagine a time when they were just one of several hundred unsigned acts schlepping around the Liverpool circuit in search of a break and without even a regular drummer.

A BRIEF HISTORY
Their first bit of luck occurred in 1960 when, having failed to secure his first three choices, Liverpool impresario, Alan Williams, booked them to play a three-month residency in Hamburg where he had an arrangement with another promoter. This also enabled them to persuade local drummer Pete Best into joining the band. It wasn't quite the showbiz opportunity they were expecting, as they found themselves playing a run down venue away from the centre and their accommodation a windowless storeroom in a nearby cinema.

After a few weeks, they were moved to a busier club in the Reeperbahn, Hamburg's red light district, where they would play up to eight hours a night to a rowdy crowd of sailors, gangsters and tourists aided by a locally available amphetamine called Preludin.

Following a dispute with a rival promoter, police were tipped off to George's underage status, and he was sent home. Then a few days later Paul and Pete were deported on a dubious charge of arson.

By all accounts they returned a different band, blowing away audiences from their first appearance at the Litherland Town Hall.

As soon as George turned 18, they went back to Hamburg where they would headline the prestigious Top Ten Club and also got to make their first official recording as backing band for Tony Sheridan on 'My Bonnie.'

Sporting new haircuts and with Paul now on bass duties*, they seemed to have taken things as far as they could, when a customer at the NEMS record store in Liverpool asked for a copy of 'My Bonnie,' prompting its manager Brian Epstein to check them out at The Cavern Club where they now had a lunchtime residency.

(*Original bassist Stu Sutcliffe had decided to remain with his new fiancee Astrid in Hamburg where, tragically, he would die of a brain haemorrhage just a few months later.)

Despite never having managed a band, he immediately offered to take them on and was soon making regular trips to London, home to all the major record labels. He'd been turned down by all of them when a cutting room engineer suggested he try George Martin, A and R head at Parlophone, an EMI subsidiary that specialised in comedy records, who was apparently looking for a strong rock 'n' roll band in order to branch out.

It's fitting they would end up on a comedy label, as according to Martin it was their sense of humour that ultimately won him over. Having got them to run through some numbers, he listed various areas he felt needed work and then asked if there was anything they didn't like.

"Well, I don't like your tie for a start," deadpanned a young George Harrison.

There was a couple of seconds silence before the room erupted. Engineer Norman Smith: "...the next fifteen to twenty minutes were pure entertainment...by the time they left, I had tears running down my face."

Martin's main concern was their drummer, one shared by the others, and a couple of days before signing the contract, Pete "unluckiest man in pop" Best was ousted in favour of Ringo, a more solid and versatile player who they also got along with much better.

Their first single 'Love Me Do' made a respectable, if not earth-shattering, Number 17. The initial contract was for two 45s with an option on EMI's part to release an album depending on their success – so a lot rested on the follow-up.

Martin wanted them to record 'How Do You Do It?' written by an independent songwriter, but John and Paul had a new track they were keen to use called 'Please Please Me'. After some re-working, Martin conceded it was superior, and six weeks later it was Number 1.

EMI picked up the option and granted them 10 hours of studio time - scheduled for their one day off supporting Helen Shapiro on her UK tour - in which they completed the entirety of the *Please, Please Me* album.

Within a month it topped the LP charts where it remained for an unprecedented 36 weeks - deposed only by their second release *With The Beatles*. The UK was now fully in the grip of Beatlemania with scenes of hysteria greeting every appearance. Despite this and three more UK Number 1s - each outselling the last - EMI's American division Capitol had yet to give them an official release.

Finally, Epstein convinced them to get behind 'I Want To Hold Your Hand,' and within three weeks it was Number 1 in the Billboard Charts, going on to sell 12 million copies worldwide.

In another of the perfectly timed coincidences that seemed to mark their rise, a few months prior to this, the host of America's biggest entertainment show Ed Sullivan saw the phenomenon first-hand when on a visit to London his plane was held up by fans awaiting their return from a Swedish TV appearance. He offered them top billing on his show, allowing them to make their US TV debut to an estimated audience of 73 million people, the highest viewing figure ever recorded. (During the broadcast, youth crime dropped to its lowest levels in decades.)

With the country emerging from the shock of the Kennedy assassination, the smiling mop-tops with the funny British accents were just what was needed to lift the collective spirit. Capitol began releasing everything they'd been sitting on, until the band that couldn't find a deal two years earlier held all of the Top 5 singles placings and a further fifteen in the Top 100 - an extraordinary feat no one has come close to matching.

They would release a further sixteen UK singles and nine more albums (all but one making the top spot) until on April 4, 1970 a statement was issued to say they were calling it a day - by which time they'd revolutionized just about every aspect of the industry, from songwriting, presentation and production to the basic business model itself.

INFLUENCE
To appreciate their impact, it helps to consider the climate in which they first appeared. With rock's pioneers either dead (Eddie Cochran, Buddy Holly, Richie Valens), disgraced (Jerry Lee Lewis, Chuck Berry) or gone soft (Elvis), the British charts were mostly filled with schmaltzy balladeers or watered-down versions of US R 'n' B hits. It was looking like the naysayers were right and rock 'n' roll really was just a passing fad.

Even by 1962 standards, 'Love Me Do' was not a sophisticated record. What it did have was a raw energy and genuine spirit - qualities long absent from the UK charts at the time. With their collarless suits and comparatively long hair, they also looked like no one else and were unusual in not having an identifiable front man - even their drummer sometimes sang lead.

As a wave of acts began copying the Beatle template, the Vince Eagers and Dickie Prides who'd been clogging up the charts found themselves looking almost instantly passé, and many watched helpless as long chart runs dried up within a few months.

Though the US scene wasn't in as bad shape, their effect was no less seismic. Sales of Vox amps and electric guitars soared following their Ed Sullivan appearance, and many of the biggest acts of the decade either formed or changed direction as a result of seeing them. Their American success also opened the door for other UK acts to break through. Prior to their arrival, only two UK acts had made the Number 1 spot - both with instrumentals. The year following 'I Want to Hold Your Hand,' the so-called "British Invasion" accounted for almost half of US chart entries.

What really marked The Beatles out was that they wrote their own material. A few US acts had done this, but it was almost unheard of in the UK, the job being assigned to staid Tin Pan Alley professionals.

As they began turning out hit after hit for others as well as themselves, acts like The Stones, The Kinks and The Who began to try their hand (Jagger and Richards started writing as a direct result of watching them finish 'I Wanna Be Your Man' in front of them - which had provided The Stones with their first big hit). Soon it wasn't just acceptable for artists to write their own material, but expected - sounding the death knell for Tin Pan Alley's dominance almost at a stroke.

The dead wood cleared, the scene was now set for the revolution that was to follow.

If 'Love Me Do' was basic, 'Please Please Me' took each element a small step forward, with more complex harmonies, a proper middle eight and with the title some wordplay. Their fourth single 'She Loves You' began unusually with the chorus, brought in the third person for the first time and ended on an exotic major $6^{th.}$. Paul McCartney said they felt especially proud of the advances made on that record, and from then on, it seems to have been a conscious decision not to repeat a trick and where possible to break some new ground with each release.

Before starting their third album *A Hard Day's Night*, EMI gave Martin access to a four-track tape machine, allowing them to create new sonic textures by double tracking vocals and adding extra instruments. Their curiosity piqued, they were soon using the studio as an instrument in itself. To satisfy their endless demands for new sounds, Martin and his engineers began pushing the equipment beyond its intended limits, deliberately over-driving inputs, rewiring speakers to act as microphones, putting vocals through rotating organ speakers, manipulating tape speeds, etc. Much of this experimentation had to be done covertly as EMI had strict rules governing recording levels and even how far a mic could be placed from the source.

Incorporating influences from anywhere and everywhere - country, soul, classical, avant garde, etc. - and the effortless ease they seemed to master any style they attempted (a legacy of their Hamburg days when they'd extended their sets with jazz standards and songs from musicals) left their contemporaries open-mouthed, and no sooner had they rewritten the rulebook, they'd torn it up again to reinvent themselves once more.

All this led to an astonishing rate of progress. Less than two years from the release of 'She Loves You,' they'd recorded 'Yesterday,' and barely a year from that had made 'Tomorrow Never Knows'.

This put pressure on other artists to experiment and progress too or risk being left behind, until it became a kind of game among the biggest acts to be the first to introduce some new instrument or effect or make their record the heaviest, longest, loudest, etc.

For perhaps the only time in history, labels actually encouraged their artists to take risks. Radio also got in on the act. It seems incredible now, but Creedence Clearwater Revival deliberately made their version of 'Suzie Q' as long as possible so as to attract airplay (it worked too - launching them to huge international success).

There was so much cross-fertilisation occurring. It's plain inaccurate to credit all of this progress to The Beatles, but the extent to which they led and galvanised the movement can be seen by the rapid slowdown in experimentation that followed their split and the sudden divergence of genres (folk, prog, glam, etc.).

HOW DID THEY DO IT?

My friend with the two shelves of Beatles books once told me the reason he thought people read so much on them was because they were looking for some kind of clue as to how they did it.

I knew what he meant, because when you look at what they achieved in the seven and a half years they were making records, it just doesn't seem possible. As well as 11/12 studio albums, 22 singles (two re-recorded in German), 13 EPs and seven fan club singles, they appeared in five feature films, made numerous TV appearances and promo clips and recorded over a hundred radio sessions. This was on top of general promotional duties including several hundred press and radio interviews. For the first half of their career they were also on tour almost constantly. Amazingly, this took precedence over recording commitments which would be squeezed in around them.

Individually they released seven solo albums, two film soundtracks (including Paul's Oscar-winning score to *The Family Way*) and either wrote, played on or produced over fifty tracks for other artists, several making Number 1. Ringo also starred in two films. John starred in one, produced several shorts, put on a couple of art exhibitions and wrote two books.

They also lent their support to various political causes, spent two months studying Transcendental Meditation in India, had to deal with various scandals and tragedies, including the furore over John's "bigger than Christ" remark, drug busts, an obscenity charge and the death of Brian Epstein leading to the legal and logistical nightmare that would be Apple, while still somehow finding the time to attend to the everyday personal stuff, getting married (twice for John), having kids, buying houses, etc.

This would be less impressive if the music didn't hold up, so check the following list: 'I Saw Her Standing There,' 'All My Loving,' 'I Should Have Known Better,' 'And I Love Her,' 'If I Fell,' 'Eight Days a Week,' 'You've Got to Hide Your Love Away,'

'Yesterday,' 'Nowhere Man,' 'Michelle,' 'Norwegian Wood,' 'Got to Get You Into My Life,' 'Good Day Sunshine,' 'With a Little Help From My Friends,' 'Lucy in the Sky With Diamonds,' 'She's Leaving Home,' 'When I'm 64,' 'Fool on the Hill,' 'Back in the USSR,' 'Ob-La-Di, Ob-La-Da,' 'While My Guitar Gently Weeps,' 'Octopus' Garden,' 'Here Comes the Sun,' 'The Long and Winding Road,' 'Across the Universe.'

You may not like all of these songs, but even if you're only a casual music fan, you'll most likely know or at least recognise all of them. Why is that remarkable?

Because not one was even a UK single.

While most acts struggle to produce one memorable song in their career, The Beatles were churning out bona fide classics on an almost daily basis. In a single 18-month period they wrote and recorded *Rubber Soul*, *Revolver* and *Sgt. Pepper* as well as three singles not included on those albums, 'Day Tripper'/'We Can Work It Out,' 'Paperback Writer'/'Rain' and what is often cited as the greatest pairing of all time: 'Strawberry Fields Forever'/'Penny Lane.'

So how did they do it? One key factor was simply how hard they worked - something they gained a reputation for from their first session, when they were the only act EMI staff saw rehearse through their lunch break. They would also be the first to work beyond midnight, becoming their standard pattern (to the irritation of their engineers).

They were also fortunate in having two primary songwriters, either of whom could have made them hugely successful. This increased both the amount they produced and its variety, with Paul's poppier, more upbeat material offering the perfect compliment to John's more downbeat, introspective stuff - a reflection of their contrasting personalities. Though it was rare for a Lennon/McCartney song post-1963 to be a genuine co-write, they continued to assist one another with their opposing natures, again helping offset the other's worst excesses (famously, John's "It couldn't get much worse" line which he contributed to Paul's 'Getting Better').

Their working methods also reflected their differing personality types. A self-confessed "lazy bastard" with a tendency to inertia, John usually worked from bursts of inspiration, becoming impatient if an idea didn't come together quickly. This was in marked contrast to Paul's disciplined, more craftsman-like approach.

Paul was also a renowned perfectionist. He would often come in early or stay behind late to work on his parts. His attention to detail was such that on 'Penny Lane' he overdubbed no less than seven separate keyboard parts, some recorded at different speeds, to subtly alter their tone, before he'd got the sound he was after. On the same song he brought in a double bassist to play one barely audible "creaking" noise to accompany the line about the banker.

Over time Paul would become their unofficial musical director (he was the only one to attend almost every session) and became known as a hard taskmaster, pushing them to do take after take if he thought they had a better one in them. This didn't always sit comfortably with the others - especially John, who'd originally formed the band. While he may not have minded sharing the limelight, it's unlikely he'd have wanted to concede it. In fact, it was his assertion they'd become "side men to Paul" he later gave as the main reason for their break-up.

During the '70s John would launch a series of bitter personal attacks on his former partner both in interview and song. These should be seen in the context of the legal battles they were going through at this time, as for the majority of their career their relationship was one of great mutual respect - Paul was the only person John deferred to musically or would entrust to finish a song if he'd lost interest or run out of ideas.

If Paul's domineering occasionally rubbed John up the wrong

way, it was the perfect antidote to his laziness, and there's no way he or the band could have achieved what they did without him. Between John's determination not to be usurped and Paul's natural workaholism and love of an artistic challenge lay the perfect formula to spur each other to ever greater heights. If either dominated an album, the other would try to reassert themselves on the next, or if some artistic breakthrough had been achieved, the other would feel compelled to match or outdo it. Thus hot on the heels of Paul's 'And I Love Her,' John came back with 'If I Fell,' while John's tribute to his Liverpool childhood 'Strawberry Fields' was quickly followed by Paul's 'Penny Lane.'

Those who believe John to have been the genius of the band should consider how some of his greatest works would have sounded minus Paul's contributions. Take away the tape loops, backwards guitar and drum patterns, all of which he provided or suggested for 'Tomorrow Never Knows', for example, and it would be half the song. Even towards the end, Paul was mainly doing what he'd always done, though this was thrown into sharper relief by having to compensate for his partner who - distracted by Yoko and a growing heroin habit - was producing much less by this point. And while John had all but given up attending sessions unless he'd written the song, Paul remained the ultimate team player, putting as much effort into his partner's work as his own.

Something else suggests they were much closer than the impression left by the post-split fall-out. Not long after first meeting, John's mother was killed in a hit-and-run accident. A year or so before that, Paul had lost his own mother to cancer. He said this created an unspoken bond between them that didn't exist before. It may also explain the emotional weight apparent even on their earliest recordings and which is lacking in many of their imitators, who sounded like boys in comparison.

Of course The Beatles were not only John and Paul. In the same way they'd relied on one another, they could not have realised their ambitions without their extraordinarily talented lead guitarist and drummer who never failed to rise to the occasion. It's hard to imagine two musicians better suited and with the ability to play in such a vast array of styles. George would also blossom into a great songwriter himself, whose work often rivalled theirs.

As important as their musical abilities was their temperament. Few would have had the patience to endure the endless re-takes or the humility to follow Paul's often exacting instructions. George was so unassuming he even gave away the solos on some of his own compositions (to Paul on 'Taxman' and Eric Clapton on 'While My Guitar Gently Weeps,') while Ringo had to be coaxed into playing his only drum solo on 'The End.'

Massive credit must also be given to George Martin. Again, it's hard to think of a producer more suited – with the open-mindedness to have let them record their own material when this was almost unheard of (and continued to be so encouraging in this endeavour), plus the technical skills to turn hummed melodies or vague instructions ("make it sound like 1,000 monks chanting," "I want to be able to smell the sawdust") into fully realised pieces.

And they may not have met him, or been signed at all, if not for the faith and dogged determination of Brian Epstein who was insisting they'd be bigger than Elvis, when they were essentially a covers band.

VICTIMS OF SUCCESS

In a way, the Beatles have become victims of their own success. Taught in music classes and quoted by trendy vicars, they will never have the cool cachet of a Doors or Velvet Underground.

Techniques they helped innovate such as ADT, flanging, close-miking, promo videos, printing lyrics on sleeves, etc., have been so copied, they're now just standard parts of the musical vocabulary, obscuring how radical they were when first introduced. Their enormous commercial success has also led to an (over-) familiarity that can breed contempt and suspicions they were pandering to it (not helped by images of them in their suits playing mainly to screaming girls).

While they made some compromises early on in terms of presentation, there would never be any concessions when it came to their music. Sexual in-jokes and early references to old age and death show a remarkable lack of regard to maintaining their fanbase given they'd started as a teen phenomenon. Lines like "I used to be cruel to my woman, I beat her and kept her apart from the things that she loved" are dark even by modern standards, and by the time of *The White Album* - in particular 'Revolution No 9' - their attitude bordered on contempt.

Such risk-taking is all the more admirable given how unappreciated much of it was. . The most ground-breaking tracks on *Help* and *Revolver* ('Ticket To Ride' and 'Tomorrow Never Knows', respectively) were voted least popular in The Beatles Book, their official fan magazine. Critics could also be disparaging, often attacking them for being 'too clever' or damning them with faint praise, e.g., the Melody Maker reviewer who found *Rubber Soul* pleasant enough, but doubted anyone would remember the songs in three months' time (!!!)

Another reason for their relative lack of credibility are the family-orientated songs they released throughout their career such as 'Yellow Submarine,' 'Octopus' Garden,' 'Ob-Bla-Di, Ob-La-Da' and the much maligned 'Maxwell's Silver Hammer.' But even here they went far beyond the call of duty, spending longer on the latter two than almost anything else they recorded, and there are some clever musical tricks within the deceptively catchy melodies (e.g., the irregular bar lengths introducing the verses on 'When I'm 64').

GOD*, THE FIFTH BEATLE?

Harvard professor-turned-acid guru Timothy Leary described The Beatles as "Divine messiahs" and "rock stars become holy men...sent by God." It might sound like LSD-induced hyperbole, but when one considers the coincidences and chance meetings with just the right people at just the right time, it's hard not to wonder if fate played a hand. Even minor idiosyncrasies worked in their favour, such as Paul's left-handedness, giving them a visual symmetry that made them the only band recognizable just from their silhouette. The mere fact four people, so talented and compatible musically, visually and mentally should grow up within a few miles of one another seems to defy the odds.

There's something so balanced and whole about their meld of personalities – Paul's innate optimism, John's pessimism/cynicism, George's spirituality, Ringo's grounded lack of pretension (who else would take a case of baked beans to the Maharishi's ashram or compare it to Butlins?) - like the four archetypes of man in one band, each containing some of the other, and capable of expressing all the aspects of the human condition, from the intellectual to the profane, the mundane to the spiritual.

The sense of (karmic?) balance seems particularly strong with John and Paul. Any quality lacking in one, the other seemed to have in spades. This is also evident in their later solo work. While often brilliant, it seemed to be crying out for the exact elements the other would have provided – a bit of edge or lyrical depth to Paul's, some melodic sweetening or a memorable bassline for John's.

It's interesting too that the song widely regarded as their pinnacle, 'A Day in the Life,' was the result of fusing two sections they'd been working on independently and which neither could complete - as if the Muse was treating them as a single entity.

But it was when the four of them played together that the real

---

*Not my school friend, the other one

magic happened. As those who saw them work observed, they could spend hours playing with sounds and switching between instruments - apparently achieving nothing. Then suddenly some force seemed to take over. The parts they'd been working on independently would all coalesce, with each knowing instinctively when to step forward or when to hold back, the so-called 'four-headed monster' thinking and acting as one.

A WORLD WITHOUT BEATLES

But if their success was purely due to luck, it's frightening to think what would have happened had any of those chance meetings or coincidences not occurred, if the customer at NEMS hadn't asked for 'My Bonnie' or the engineer who recommended George Martin had been on his lunch break.

Because not only might we not have all of their music, but probably also that of The Stones*, The Who, The Kinks, The Yardbirds, The Byrds, The Lovin' Spoonful, The Mamas and the Papas, The Monkees, Crosby, Stills and Nash, etc. - and certainly not in the same form.

(*As well providing them with their first big hit and inspiring them to write, The Stones were signed to Decca on George's recommendation.)

Even acts that weren't overtly Beatle-esque were often influenced in some form. Motown producers would check every Beatles release to see where they were up to sonically. John Cale said The Velvet Underground had to "completely rethink our game" after hearing 'Norwegian Wood.'

There's also the countless acts who came later, and again, it's not just the obvious ones. German experimentalists Can formed after hearing 'I Am The Walrus,' Ozzy Osbourne said Paul was his idol and called them "the Mozarts of our time," The Ramones named themselves after Paul's stage name in Hamburg, Lemmy's favourite album is *Please Please Me*, Kurt Cobain said they were his favourite band, Gilby Clarke of Guns and Roses said Lennon was his favourite writer, Brian May said Queen saw them as their "Bible." You'd be hard pushed to find a major band that doesn't include at least one obsessive.

And it wasn't just the musical landscape they changed. For better or worse, their use of cannabis and LSD encouraged millions to experiment, and when they renounced drugs in favour of meditation, it played a major part in bringing spiritual practices to the West.

I MUST BE IN LOVE
I realise too that it's also because of people like me gushing on about them in quasi-mystical terms that many are put off. But I can't help it. To me they really were perfect. I love how even their mistakes were taken to the extreme and seem somehow essential to the "plan."

For example, I can't stand 'Revolution No 9'. To me it's eight minutes of self-indulgent, migraine-inducing cacophony. But I love that it exists and that the most unlistenable track of the era was made by the same band that produced 'She Loves You.'

Or Apple. Not just a slightly naive attempt to create a utopian business empire, but the embodiment of faith over reason, that would fall into such disarray it would end up almost bankrupting them, leading to the hiring of Allen Klein (probably the most unscrupulous manager in rock history) and a betrayal of all its ideals that would take five years of intense legal wranglings to untangle.

While I'm personally in the camp that thinks Yoko was a controlling, manipulative nightmare, I love her part in the story and that she has literally become the byword for nightmarish, controlling wives/girlfriends.

Though a part of me wishes they'd continued making music, I'm also pleased they broke up when they did, at the top of their game, all looking great and before any of them had even turned 30 (George was just 27 when they split!). And it almost had to end in such bitter acrimony so they could never spoil the myth with some disappointing come-back album or embarrassing reunion concert.

There's a couple of things I'm not wild about – rhyming "two" with "two" on the middle eight of 'Do You Want to Know a Secret' and the Hammond organ on 'Mr Moonlight.' But for me, their only out-and-out fuck-up was on *Abbey Road*.

The final track was intended to be 'The End.' However, an engineer who'd been instructed to keep everything they recorded tacked a discarded version of 'Her Majesty' to the end of the master reel. When Paul heard this come on unexpectedly, he liked the effect and decided to keep it. Had he stuck to the original plan, their last album would have ended with the lines: "And in the end, the love you take is equal to the love you make" - about the most perfect coda to their career I could think of.

I guess they were human after all.

(This essay was expanded on after its initial writing. See also 'End Notes.')

CHELSEA, SQUATTING AND A VERY BAD DAY

Sat 14 Oct 2006

Today is my birthday. As I haven't had a full day off since starting these essays, I had an idea for a short one about how I ended up at the Live Aid concert which I thought I could knock off in about half an hour, leaving me the rest of the day to lounge around doing as little as possible.

But then Amie called to say something had come up in Australia that meant she may have to go back there, possibly for good. As usual, she wouldn't go into details, so it was hard to know what to say. Later I began thinking about how she likes silly stories, especially if they involve some kind of misfortune, so I decided I'd write an essay for her to read on the plane about an extremely messy tour I went on, ending with one particularly awful day, that would hopefully make her smile and take her mind off things for a bit.

I don't mind doing this in the circumstances, but I'm buggered if I'm spending my birthday writing two essays, so I'm going to include it here instead of the Live Aid one, plus some pre-amble linking it to the essay about coming to London, as it follows from there and helps set the scene. I was thinking of including it here at some point, so it's not entirely selfless, but come on, cut me some slack here. It's my fucking birthday.

A few days before Nick and I had to leave the Latimer Road flat, I had a visit from Garry who I knew from the comp I went to in Crowborough. He was looking to move up and had been given the address of someone on the Old Kent Road called Dave who apparently opened squats for people if he thought they were deserving. I was still unsure about the whole squatting thing, but Garry said his brother had done it for a while and you were usually safe as long as you stuck to council-owned property. (The way the squatting laws worked at the time was that as long as a property was unoccupied and you weren't caught breaking in, the only way to evict you was through the civil courts - a process that could take anything from a couple of months to a couple of years, depending on the efficiency of the courts - during which you got to live there for nothing. Squatters tended to avoid private property in case the owners sent in the heavies, whereas councils usually did things by the book.)

Dave offered to help and said there was an empty flat in a nearby estate that would probably suit our needs. He recommended going for it that afternoon as people were less likely to report noises and bangs during the daytime. We went to buy a lock while he gathered some tools and a 'London Borough of Southwark' workman's jacket he told us he once nicked from a roadworks.

The block was called Wendover House, one of several in the sprawling Aylesbury Estate. It only took Dave a few seconds to crowbar the door, and while he set to work fitting the lock, we inspected our new home - a spacious mezzanine with lots of natural light. Our only concern was the estate itself which had a distinctly edgy vibe. As if to confirm our fears, a neighbour appeared at the door. He didn't care that we were squatting. He was more curious why we'd chosen this particular building and then mentioned he'd been broken into no less than thirteen times in the previous two years.

The next day I started ferrying my stuff from Latimer Road. As

I entered the estate, I literally had to run to escape a pack of dogs that appeared to be living wild. It was the sort of thing you might expect in the slums of Rio, but Camberwell?

On my second trip I got into the lift where there was a puddle of piss and what looked like a human turd. A woman then entered and on seeing my bags asked if I was moving in or out.

"In," I said.

"Oh," she replied. "You'll hate it here."

It was now dark, and Garry and I were both starving. If the estate felt edgy by day, at night it was fucking terrifying. Eventually we mustered the courage to go to a chip shop about five minutes away, and even on that short journey we witnessed a cab being done over by a gang of kids.

The next day I returned to Latimer Road and ran into Nick. When he heard my description of the place, he arranged for me to join him on the floor of a student flat, rented by another ex-Downsider, a Japanese guy called Simon.

While chatting with Dave, he'd mentioned a couple of upmarket squatted blocks including a half-squatted one called Moravian Towers right on the King's Road, SW3. It sounded almost mythical, but it was real, and by total chance I'd ended up in it.

It was co-owned by the Royal Borough of Kensington and Chelsea and Chelsea Arts College (where Simon was studying). They were trying to clear it to sell on to developers, but usually within a couple of weeks of one becoming vacant, someone would pull off the boarding, kick the door open and take it. In a few cases the original tenants had let themselves in with their old keys to continue living in the same flat, but now for free.

We spent about three months at Simon's when he finally got sick of us abusing his hospitality and said we had three days to move out. Luckily, a flat had become free on the floor above, so armed with my basic squatting knowledge, I moved in with Paul (the friend I hooked up with when I arrived in London). Nick had finally been thrown off his college course by this point so decided to leave London altogether. We were then joined by Jim, one of Simon's legitimate flatmates who wanted to save on rent, and then an American girl I'd started seeing called Julie, who had to leave her accommodation after finishing a college course.

About four months later we received our eviction notice and moved to a bigger flat two floors below, with two more ex-Downside guys Mark and Jaz. When that came to an end, we broke into a place literally across the hall - the easiest flat move I ever made.

Someone could write a great book about Moravian as it became the centre of a legal stand-off between squatters and the RBK and C.

If I had the time, I'd tell you about the two dealer flats locked in a price war, ensuring we had the cheapest prices in town, and almost every flat you'd enter would be thick with smoke, and reggae was constantly blasting.

Then there were the various mad, bad and sometimes hilarious characters the place seemed to magnetically attract, like the diplomat's son who could legally carry drugs due to his father's immunity, Christian Jennings (yet another ex-Downsider) who said he'd done a runner from the French Foreign Legion (he later wrote a book about his experiences) or the recently divorced lorry driver who Mark took pity on and after staying just one night managed to stink the place up so badly we moved out three weeks before our actual court date.

But it looked like the party was finally coming to an end. The council had got wise to our tactics, and instead of the flimsy bits of plywood they'd been nailing across the fronts, were now welding solid steel frames almost the moment one became empty. Luckily, I'd begun renting a cheap room on a nearby houseboat for Julie and I to move into if/when they finally shut the place.

During this time I'd been working as a barman at the old Marquee Club on Wardour Street. We were allowed in for free on our nights off, so as often as I could I'd check who was playing in the hope of finding a good band that looked like it could use another guitarist and/or some songs.

One night I came to see a punk band called Chelsea. They'd been going for a few years and were mainly known for a punk anthem and John Peel favourite called 'Right To Work.' Their career never fully recovered after NME ran a blacked-out photo their singer Gene October once did for a gay porno mag, but I remember a friend saying he really liked their first album and that they were very underrated.

I wasn't so impressed by the band, but I thought Gene was great - a true showman more in the spirit of people like Jim Morrison or Iggy Pop than the typical punk types. During one song he'd started getting increasingly pissed off about something, though it wasn't clear what. He began shouting at the other players and then half-way through the next song threw his mic down and stormed off through a door at the side of the stage.

The band started giving each other "what's going on?" looks, while playing the same riff round and round. Just as they looked ready to give up, Gene came bounding back onstage with a huge grin and a football under his arm. He kicked it into the crowd, then launched into the final chorus – sending the room nuts, as everyone realised the whole thing was a wind-up not even the band was in on.

With the punk scene on its last legs, I started thinking if I could get myself in there and push the band in a more Stonesy direction - where I felt sure Gene's heart truly lay - it could work to everyone's advantage.

Gene sometimes drank at the Marquee bar, so the next time I saw him, I asked if he was interested in a second guitarist. "I might be," he said. "You're not a songwriter by any chance?" He explained they were due to start recording an album soon and were a couple of songs short.

The next day he came by the squat. The first thing he did was look through my records and pulled out all the Stones' ones. I then played him some songs I thought might suit, and he told me I was in. He said to come to their next gig to meet the others, and a few days later we started recording the album. Considering we had five days to do it and I hadn't even played with them when I went in, I thought it came out well.

They ended up using four of my songs (which we had to work out in the studio), plus one called 'The Amazing Adventures of Frank Hoblin' that our producer Dave Goodman put forward as he thought it would fit the semi-psychedelic new direction. Two of my songs, 'Valium Mother' and 'Monica, Monica' were chosen for the single (Gene even kept my guide vocal on the latter). It received a good review in Melody Maker (who compared it to Steely Dan of all people), while the album got a rave in Sounds from someone who said he'd previously hated the band. Of the four tracks he named as stand-outs, three were mine and the other was 'Amazing Adventures.'

The new direction seemed to be working out. We played a four-Friday residency at the Fulham Greyhound, and then it was off for a twenty-date European tour to promote the *Original Sinners* album.

For the first time ever, everything in my life was going to plan. Aside from the music, I had a pretty American girlfriend and not one, but two addresses in Chelsea. The next time I returned to Crowborough, it would be with my head held high and a rock 'n' roll swagger in my step. But pride comes before a fall, and within a month nearly all of it had turned to shit.

After a rough ferry crossing, we arrived in Sweden and immediately set off to Bergen in Norway for the first date of the tour. It was winter, so this meant around 300 miles of snow-covered mountain roads in a transit van packed with gear and six people (including our driver/roadie Tony).

For much of the way there were no barriers and a drop on one side of several hundred feet. Many of the roads were barely wide enough for two vehicles. This didn't bother some of the lorry drivers who'd regularly come hurtling around a corner, forcing both drivers to slam on the brakes, and then one would have to pull in hard to the side so the other could pass.

Every mile or two you'd see some burnt-out vehicle submerged in one of the frozen lakes or wrapped around a tree halfway down - a reminder that even if you somehow survived the fall, you'd either burn, drown or freeze to death. There was other crazy stuff like long, unlit tunnels full of black ice and roads with rocks jutting from the sides at windscreen level which you'd have to swerve to avoid.

It was the most terrifying journey of my life, and I spent most of it with my fingers digging into my palms. Just as we'd made it round some hairpin bend and thought we'd seen the worst of it, there'd be some snaking road stretched out ahead and yet more horrors to confront.

When at last we got to Bergen, we realised we'd gone through all of this to play to a seated crowd of about thirty students following some book reading. And there was still the return journey to face.

About a half hour after leaving Bergen, we skidded on some ice in one of the unlit tunnels, sending the van spinning. It was about to tip over when we hit a wall, knocking us back upright. We shoved some amps back into place and then drove out before a lorry ploughed into us.

About twenty minutes later we approached a narrow wooden bridge with a juggernaut coming towards us from the other side. It didn't look wide enough for both vehicles, but neither driver was giving way. At the last second there was a loud screech as both hit the brakes. We were okay, but it was close enough to knock in our mirrors.

We eventually made it to Oslo in one piece for our second gig. The venue looked good this time and was soon filled with a hardcore crowd of tattooed and mohicanned punks, with some passing around bags of glue to sniff from. Punk was still being taken very seriously in what would become the home of satanic metal and ritual church burnings.

We started to notice a growing tension in the room that felt like it was aimed at us, though no one could figure out why. When it came time to play, Gene ran to the mic and shouted, "We're Chelsea from the UK, and we're the best fucking band you lot will ever see" - his usual crowd-baiting style, while Tim (aka "Phoenix") began the riff to our set opener 'Two More Hours.'

Suddenly a pint glass came flying through the air and shattered against the wall behind us. Then another came, this one breaking against the neck of Tim's guitar. I considered running off, but luckily that was the end of it, and the atmosphere gradually calmed.

Later, someone explained the reason for the trouble. Earlier, someone had asked Gene if his band could play a short set before ours and he'd told him to fuck off. It then went round we'd snubbed this local band (not the punk spirit) and also that the guy was dying from cancer and it was one of his ambitions to play with us. (I don't know if that was true, but it was what went round.) So Gene then coming on and basically telling them how lucky they were to have us was the final insult.

A couple of days later we were strip-searched at the German border and Tim was caught with 7 grams of speed down his trousers. They decided to let him off with a "fine," but there were a worrying couple of hours where we thought we might have to complete the tour without him.

The tour continued in this vein with drinking matches, a police raid and the usual tour "shenanigans" (Julie had agreed to me sleeping around while I was away, which I was determined to make the most of).

Some of the gigs were good, but none of my songs had been added to the set, including the single. There were simmering tensions from the others, who'd eyed me with suspicion ever since I was foisted on them, and because of a credit on the album saying 'all songs by Tim Briffa and Chelsea' which they thought I'd somehow engineered, a notion the ever shit-stirring Gene did nothing to dispel.

After three weeks of getting hammered every night, waking up a couple of hours later to cram into a van alongside five others all sweating out their previous night's toxins and also feeling like bags of shit, then driving a couple of hundred miles to the next gig to do it all over again, we were all paying the price. I'd also noticed a worrying stinging pain every time I took a piss. I wondered if Julie's forgiving nature would extend to me returning with a sexually transmitted disease.

But I promised to tell you about my very bad day - the last of the tour. I'm counting it from waking up to when I next went to sleep, though in reality this was closer to two days.

It began with an alarm call and finding myself in a German Holiday Inn-type hotel room. Along with the nausea and shakes that were by now standard was that awful sense of free-floating anxiety you get when you know something terrible happened the night before but you can't remember what. I then noticed various cuts and bruises over my body. I went to the bathroom mirror and saw a big emerging black eye. I started to recall some kind of fight and possibly being kicked in the head at one point, but I couldn't remember who it was with or what it was about. I managed to get dressed and went to the reception where I saw Tony and Geoff, our drummer. They were most amused by my state, and when they realised I had no memory of what led to it, took great pleasure in filling me in.

The fight was with our bass player Pete over a girl he was after that I'd ended up with. Not the first time, they said, which had apparently been adding to the tensions. At some point I may also have called him "a gorilla." We started exchanging blows as we were getting into the van to leave the club and were still at it when we got back to the hotel. It had taken us about half an hour to get there, so it must have been pretty epic. We were in the lobby still going strong (this was when Pete began kicking me in the head) when the hotel manager came to investigate and finally broke it up – this despite Gene trying to talk him out of it by saying we were "mates just having a laugh."

The fight seemed to clear the air with me and Pete, and we actually ended up going to breakfast together and laughing about it. We then all set off to Dieppe for our final gig.

For some reason, someone decided to spend the previous night's gig money on a big ball of hash which almost no one had touched due to how fucked up we'd all got. There were three borders to get to Dieppe, so the sensible thing would have been to throw it away. Of course, we decided to chance it, and to split the risk, divided it between me, Pete, Geoff and Tony. (As always, Gene refused to carry any, and we excused Tim as he was driving.)

Our support band was driving in front of us, and at the first border they were pulled over, while we were told to wait. As the border police were looking into their van, we started getting more nervous. We'd already all put our lumps into our mouths when Geoff announced "I don't know about you guys, but I'm swallowing mine," and one by one we all did the same.

Not only did they end up waving us through, but a couple of minutes later someone pointed out we'd just entered Holland, where of course hash was legal. For some reason I've never got high from eating dope, but the others were soon flying. As you can imagine, it wasn't the tightest of gigs.

We'd all been saying how we couldn't wait to get back to our own beds, and as the ferry port was close by and Tim had got himself some speed, he offered to do the whole journey back that night.

We got to Dover, then drove up to Stafford where Pete, Geoff and Tony lived (and who were all still off their heads when he dropped them off), and around midday we began the last leg down to London.

I was in the back trying to get some sleep when I heard Gene say something about a cute-looking hitchhiker. The van slowed, and in stepped a guy who'd had the bed next to me at Downside. "All right, Phil!"

By the time I got to Moravian, I just wanted to sleep for as long as I could, but the first thing I saw was our eviction notice dated just a couple of weeks away. I'd gone back to signing on after joining the band, and there was also a letter from the dole office requesting an interview. At the top someone had written in biro 'ex. Passport,' which I assumed was short for 'examine passport.' (I'd neglected to mention I was going abroad which at the time meant a potential jail term and at the least having your benefits stopped.)

At least we had the room on the houseboat. When Julie appeared, I suggested we go to tell the landlord we'd soon be properly moving in, but when we got there, we found a girl in the room who said she'd just moved in. When the landlord showed up, he told me he'd let it to her as I'd missed the last month's rent and he'd been unable to contact me. I said I'd paid it before I left. He got out the rent book. "Shit, you're right." I asked who got to keep the room.

"Seeing as she's already moved her stuff in...I'm sorry, man."

As well as being severely sleep deprived and aching all over from the fight, I was facing imminent homelessness, no income and possibly prison, and I was almost certain my days in the band were numbered. And I still had to tell Julie I had an STD.

I then did something I thought only happened in movies - and burst into hysterical laughter.

THE FIVE CATEGORIES OF RELATIONSHIP

Sun 15 Oct 2006

By the time I finished writing yesterday's essay it was around 10pm. I thought I should do something for my birthday, so I rang our bassist Dave and we ended up at a club in Old Street called Catch.

I was at the bar when a pretty brunette walked in. I shouted, "Oi, you! What do you want to drink?" ('Instinctive Approach.') She looked me up and down and then asked for a neat vodka. She was with a friend, so I bought her a drink, then introduced them to Dave, and luckily we all hit it off.

After Catch closed, we found another bar where Lou (the brunette) grabbed my hand - which I wasn't expecting. Later we took a cab to mine, listened to Booker T and the MGs and the Velvet Underground and then went to bed. So it was a good birthday after all.

We spent this afternoon hanging out and at one point got into a discussion about divorce and failed relationships. I said a relationship was usually doomed the moment a guy lost his hard-on for the girl, to which Lou replied, "But don't men always lose interest - sooner or later?" I said it depended on the category of relationship and that there were five basic types. "Which are?"

THE FIVE CATEGORIES OF RELATIONSHIP:

TYPE 1: This is where you have sex with someone just once, and almost the second it's over wish you hadn't. Usually the result of desperation and/or opportunism ("it was there," "filth on a plate"). Type 1s usually involve copious amounts of alcohol, so while you'd like to leave or kick her out if it's your place, you will most likely just roll over for a few hours of sticky, interrupted sleep. When you awake, dry-mouthed and head pounding, you will attempt conversation, but with no real chemistry between you, and with the few topics of mutual interest already exhausted the previous night, this will only add to the awkwardness.

Though by now all you want is to be rid of this person forever, you may yet find yourself asking her number in a rather desperate attempt to conceal the fact you've basically used her for sex, and while she realises this, she will probably still give it.

When finally you are alone, you will take a long shower to remove the smell of sweat and incompatible pheromones. The self-disgust is not so easily removed.

TYPE 2: These are based on real chemistry and attraction and survive the first sexual encounter with no sudden loss of interest. Passions will start to diminish however, after the second or third encounter, and by the fifth all genuine desire will be gone.

Depending on one's libido, it may be possible to continue things for a while longer, but faced with the physical evidence of your waning enthusiasm, even she will have to accept defeat sooner or later. It's common for some sexual desire to return after a few weeks apart, but one must resist the temptation to suggest another date, as this will be just when she is starting to recover from the blow to her self-esteem, and there's no better way to complete the process than by rejecting the person who dealt it.

TYPE 3: Also based on genuine chemistry and attraction, these make it past the fifth encounter with no obvious loss of interest. But there will also be no increase - the defining characteristic of a

Type 3 being that it hits an early peak where it remains.

Men often like a relationship based mainly on having a good time and which basically just cruises, and she may enjoy it too, initially, but the female instinct to "take things on to the next level" usually kicks in at some point. So while it tends to be the man who ends a Type 2 relationship, it's normally the woman who ends a Type 3, as soon as she realises it's not really going anywhere - typically between three to nine months in.

TYPE 4: Instead of plateauing, a Type 4 relationship continues to develop on both a sexual and emotional level. But there will still be incompatibilities which can never be fully resolved, until one must eventually choose between ending it or a life of constant compromise and good, but rarely amazing, sex. (Around 2½ years/1,000 days in is usually when problems start to come to a head.)

Ending it will likely be painful as by now you will have a couple of years worth of shared experiences, references to obscure late-night TV shows you caught together and private jokes no one else will understand. There may also be a fear you're throwing away your best shot at happiness to pursue an idealised version of love that may only exist in Hollywood and romantic fiction.

As ever, one's decision will be strongly influenced by how much other choice you have, and it may be worth tolerating a less-than-perfect relationship if the alternative is being on your own or a worse one.

TYPE 5: This is the relationship you hoped/suspected of existing, aka "the One," "true" love, falling "in" love," etc. I've already discussed this subject in the 'How to Pick Up Girls Pt. 2' essay, so all I'll add here is that a Type 5 survives all the key danger points with no serious problems. The relationship may become more companion-like after the 2½ year/1,000-night point, but tends to remain strong. They may yet break down (six to seven years seems to be a common danger point), but in most cases this seems more to do with wanting a fresh experience than there being something fundamentally wrong.

DIFFICULTIES WITH THE THEORY
Clearly, not all relationships fall neatly into these time frames, but I would argue they still inherently belong to one of the five categories, but were either brought to a premature end for some reason, e.g., parental disapproval, having to move country or they were extended beyond their natural lifespan for convenience, fear of being alone, etc., in which case a typical Type 3 could outlast a Type 4 or even a 5.

The most common reason a relationship becomes artificially prolonged is marriage, especially in cultures that forbid divorce and/or premarital sex. I shudder to think how many people have spent their wedding night realising they'll have to live out their days with a Type 1.

Just as some Buddhists believe all life-forms have a pre-determined number of breaths, it's also possible that rather than chronological time, what determines the length of a relationship is how many times you have sex (as with categories 1 and 2). I haven't fully made my mind up on that one.

As usual when offering my theories, I only gave Lou a condensed version. I then asked if it fitted with her own experiences - allowing for the personal/male perspective.

"I'd have to think about that," she said, and then after a few seconds, "...so where are we then?"

I wasn't expecting such a direct question or what the answer was. Although we'd "fooled around," we hadn't yet had full sex, so potentially we could be a Type 1. However, we were now both sober and still getting on, so a Type 2 or maybe a 3 seemed more likely. I doubted we'd make it to 4, and I know we're not a 5. But the real question was whether to tell her this. If I wasn't careful, we might not even make it to 1.

Before I had a chance to put my foot in it, Lou then clarified, "...I mean in relation to transport. I have to get back to Shoreditch at some point."

I said the tube was probably her best option and I'd walk her to the station whenever she wanted.

DOWNSIDE

Mon 16 Oct 2006

Whatever I felt about Holmewood, it was like a holiday camp compared to my next school, Downside. Based around an order of Catholic monks in the heart of Somerset, I'd been dreading the place for years. My brothers had all been, and though they tended to be (conspicuously) quiet on the subject during holidays, I would read their occasional letters home telling of their homesickness and tales of compulsory boxing matches, widespread bullying and theft. I remember one about a kid whose parents had sent him a watch for his birthday. It was immediately taken off him by two others boys who used it in a quick, makeshift game of tennis and then handed back to him in bits.

The school also operated the "fagging" system. If you're unfamiliar, this is an old public school tradition where sixth formers are assigned a junior boy to carry out chores and errands, anything from cleaning their rugby boots to stealing food for them from the kitchens (and being expected to take the blame if caught). Compounding my gloom, I'd recently caught a TV adaptation of *Tom Brown's Schooldays* that included a particularly grim scene where arch-bully Flashman decides to "roast the fag" as punishment for some minor crime and poor Tom is made to stand in front of an open fire in his short trousers until he grows tired of his whimpering.

The place was as depressing as I'd imagined, full of tall, looming spires and endless drafty halls and corridors. I found my bed near the end of a long dormitory and watched a succession of spotty arses changing into their pyjamas - already hating the place and most of the people in it. Not everyone was feeling miserable. In fact some of the boys seemed to be having a great old time, jumping between beds, shouting, "Tomasss!" or, "Jonesey!!" at one another. I formed a particular dislike towards these people and later discovered many already knew each other, having come from the same prep schools. The only person I knew was a guy from my hometown whose dad worked with mine and had arranged for us to meet the previous holidays so we'd both know at least one person when we got there.

The next day a monk gave us a tour of the grounds that included a trip to the top of the abbey. Pointing to one of the playing fields, he told us how in World War Two a couple of fighter planes were returning from some mission, and seeing a crowd watching some school match, decided to show off with an aerial display of "follow-my-leader." The first plane did a "loop-the-loop," which the second plane tried to copy but didn't quite pull off and ended up killing nine boys and badly injuring another dozen.

The following evening the senior part of the school arrived, and then the term started in earnest. It was a full-on schedule, starting with a House assembly at 8am, then breakfast, lessons from 9 to 1pm (with a half hour break at 11), lunch, sports, tea, another set of lessons from 4.30pm to 7, dinner and then a final study period from 8 to 9.15pm - leaving 45 minutes to get ready for lights out at 10pm. That was from Mon to Fri. Lessons ran to 1pm on a Saturday, leaving the rest of the day free (assuming you weren't roped into some cross-country run or having to support some team). Sunday was free apart from an hour's mass in the morning.

When you have 600 teenage boys having to work, sleep and shit next to each other for weeks on end, tensions inevitably develop. It was particularly bad among the new boys as many were used to being top dog at their previous school. Now that we were all at the bottom of the pile, little gangs and cliques started forming as everyone tried to reassert their status.

I'd mainly been hanging out with some people I'd met on the train down and the guy from my town. Being introduced turned out to be a mixed blessing as he'd been head chorister at his previous school and made the mistake of boasting about it. It wasn't long before the obvious jibes started up. Sensing trouble, the people around him began to distance themselves, a couple even joining in.

He'd been nice to me, and I wasn't going to desert him just because of these cowardly pricks. So then I started getting it. Soon we were both having our beds stripped at least once a day and getting constantly challenged to fight. I could never seem to back down from one, even when the guy was clearly much tougher. Consequently, I averaged a fight a week that term and took a couple of bad pummellings - one guy broke his hand on me, and I had to deal with other shit like having a thumbscrew put on me and being held down by three guys in the school pool. It still wasn't as bad as what some were getting. I saw beds being pissed in and all kinds of degrading stuff they're probably still in therapy for.

Refusing to back down paid off in the end, as I found people usually left you alone after that - sometimes even giving you a grudging respect for at least having stood up to them, and by the end of the term I seemed to have settled it with everyone.

The bullying dealt with, my second term was less traumatic, if a long way from enjoyable. As Junior House members, we had no access to TV and just two ping-pong and one (soon-ripped) snooker table for entertainment. Occasionally, someone would buy alcohol from the nearby village - a military-style operation involving uniform changes and running the gauntlet of the locals who naturally hated us. An easier and cheaper option was to get high off various aerosols and thinners, and there was a dangerous craze in that for a while.

Porn was also rife. I was on a big guilt trip about this thanks to various talks and sermons warning of the temptations of the flesh. One left a big enough impression that I can still recite some of it.

"...And if your right eye causes you to sin, I say to you, pluck it out! For it is better to go through life missing an eye than to burn for all eternity in the fires of Hell. And if your right hand causes you to sin, cut it off! For it is better to go through life missing a hand than to burn for all eternity..."

I was always amazed how some people could just shrug this stuff off, like Paul (the guy I hooked up with when I first came to London), who would smuggle German hardcore mags into Mass and read them from behind his hymn book.

Vandalism was another popular past-time. If it involved some kind of loud bang or explosion, all the better. People would be constantly letting off fire extinguishers or blowing stuff up with cherry bombs, and there was barely a room in the school without at least a couple of its smaller windowpanes broken. As the school left most repairs until the holidays, come winter the place became absolutely freezing. I'd spend whole break periods huddled against a radiator or sitting in a boiler room where they dried our laundry. Once a window was broken in my dormitory, and a couple of nights I had to sleep with snow actually blowing onto my bed. If anyone complained about the Arctic conditions, they were told the laws governing minimum temperatures didn't apply to private schools, the same reason they were allowed to cane us.

One of the biggest frustrations was that the school had just added an extra year to the O Level curriculum. As almost nothing we'd been taught was even on the syllabus, this was seen as a way to squeeze and extra year's worth of fees from the parents and meant the entire first year had basically been a waste of time.

The school had also just changed the uniform to a dull grey suit.

Unlike the previous pinstripe, you could only buy the new one from the school's own tailor, another earner for the monks. As a concession to anyone like myself who'd had elder brothers at the school, we were allowed to wear their handed down pinstripes if we chose. But we soon realised whenever one of us sent ours to be cleaned, the tailor would always manage to 'lose' it. So you had no choice but to buy the new one off him. He became so brazen, one guy who took a pair of trousers for repair had them scissored in front of him.

Something I did like about the school was that you had to learn an instrument for your first year, so I chose guitar. They were supposed to teach us classical, but the school used an outside teacher who'd played in various rock bands in the '60s and '70s, and between the obligatory 'Greensleeves' and scales, he'd show me the riffs to 'Day Tripper' and 'The Last Time.' His Friday lesson was about the only time I felt sane, and I'd spend the whole week looking forward to them.

Along with the World War Two plane crash story was another that was a big part of the school lore. I heard a few versions, all a bit different, but the basic gist was that a few years before some boys were messing around with a Ouijah board and got through to the spirit of a monk who'd been kicked out of the school for some reason. At some point they asked for a prediction, and the glass spelled out "death." Then a load of strange stuff happened with windows flying open and a statue of St John Robert in a nearby dormitory appearing to move and glow, while several boys threw up. The statue was taken away to be exorcised and the whole school ordered to take confession. One boy didn't go and was later killed in an odd car crash in which all the other passengers survived.

If it sounds like typical schoolboy imaginings, there's reason to think at least some of it was true. Dom Philip Jebb who'd supposedly carried out the exorcism did perform them from time to time, and the other monks were also very cagey on the subject, neither confirming nor denying it happened. The alcove that housed the statue was also still empty, though the plaque bearing the Saint's name remained. I can vouch for this personally as I was moved to Roberts House at the start of my second year and had to sleep a few meters from it.

It so happened Jebb took over as Headmaster that year. With his silver hair, piercing blue eyes and strange high-pitched voice, he was just how you might imagine an exorcist monk. He was also rumoured to be able to read minds. This I'm more sceptical of, but it was widely believed and all added to his fearsome reputation.

On his second assembly, Jebb announced he was reducing the number of times we could leave the school grounds to just twice a term. The next week he raised the smoking fine from £1 to £10. He then ruled the dormitories were out of bounds during the daytime - supposedly to reduce thieving. If anything, it made it easier for thieves, and as you didn't get a room until the sixth form, the majority of the school now had to spend our free time hanging around corridors or wandering aimlessly from one empty classroom to the next.

Each week he'd introduce some draconian new rule, until about halfway through the term he said he was banning "noise machines" - radios, record players, etc., for everyone apart from prefects.

We all relied on music to stay sane, and almost immediately word went round of a protest. A few days later at midnight, someone rang the school bell and almost the whole school ran into the main quad in our dressing gowns and began lobbing the loo rolls we'd been collecting and chanting for Jebb to resign. In a rare act of solidarity, even the prefects joined in.

The "Downside Riot" made the Daily Telegraph who said it could be heard in a neighbouring town. The next assembly Jebb said he'd taken our feelings on board and that we could keep our "noise machines."

It was a clever political move, making us feel like we'd won some victory while conceding almost nothing. The other rules stayed in place, and life continued as before.

The second year was also when I began my fagging duties. Compared to some, my Fag-master wasn't too bad, and I mostly just had to make him and his friends tea each break. He rarely bought tea or sugar, though, so by the time I'd scrounged some and waited for one of the two House kettles to be free, I'd be lucky to have ten minutes for myself.

The misery was unrelenting. Unlike Holmewood, we weren't forced to eat the food. If we were served something that almost no one ate, rather than throw it away, the cooks would often reheat it and serve it for the next meal. Depending on the next meal, you could go a couple of days on nothing apart from cereal at breakfast and bread or a small cake for tea.

This had happened during a bad flu outbreak that quickly filled up the sick bays and at one point confined me and around half the school to our dormitories, so we were both ill and starving. A boy happened to pass ours holding a packet of digestives. Someone shouted out for one, and as he wasn't allowed in the dorm, he chucked it towards him. Others started asking for one and he ended up chucking biscuits all around the dorm, and we were pulling each other aside just to get broken bits off the floor.

Another issue were "quads" - the main system of punishment. This meant a change into your gym kit before breakfast on a Tuesday and then about a mile run to the pavilion and back for every five you'd been given. Prefects could award them, and there was never a shortage of fascist pricks who'd dole them out on a whim. If they asked your name, people would sometimes give that of another boy, usually one of the bullying victims. As you weren't allowed to challenge them, this meant they'd regularly be running 10-15 quads a week they hadn't even earned, on top of everything else they were dealing with.

This was all widely known, but the monks turned a blind eye, just as they did to the freezing temperatures, corrupt tailor and all the other shit.

There were always a few mad fuckers who just didn't give a shit, and it was great whenever they got one over the monks. Once they'd allowed some boys to set up a shortwave radio station for the school, but then had to shut it down when one of the DJs was discovered reading stories from Penthouse as part of his late-night show.

In retrospect, I wish I'd rebelled more. I didn't, mainly so as not to upset my parents who'd sacrificed a lot to send me there unaware of how much the school had gone downhill (it had once been known as "the Catholic Eton").

Aside from playing music, I mainly channelled my energies into various practical jokes and wind-ups which I'd plot with a Canadian friend called Chris. We pulled off some good ones. At some point we'd been granted a study room with a desk space each which people would personalise with posters and drapes. One guy built this elaborate wooden frame around his with a set of curtains hanging off. While he was away, Chris and I used a Swiss Army penknife to saw about 2/3 through each bit of wood, then tied a piece of string around them leading to a "trip-wire" across the entrance, so when he got back, the entire thing collapsed on top of him. Another time we convinced a notorious hypochondriac he was losing his memory just by getting a few people to say, "Not that story again," or, "You've told me that twice already," every time he said something.

Had it not been for the extra year, I'd have had my own room after my second year and might have survived two more, but I was now going seriously stir crazy.

During one set of holidays, I'd started playing with a drummer from my town called Richard. He suggested I finish my studies at the local comp he went to, which he said was very relaxed as well as co-ed (the other big frustration). I began calling my parents every weekend, begging them to let me switch, until eventually they agreed. It was like a reprieve from prison.

I knew it would take a lot for the monks to expel me, when I'd be leaving soon anyway, so I then began a quiet campaign of revenge against the various injustices and stuff I'd hated.

Everyone agreed the quad system was unfair and we should at least be able to challenge any blatantly unfair ones, so I set about organising a mass boycott. A lot of people said they'd join in, but come the day, I was the only to keep to it. Instead of being punished, my quads were simply moved to the following week, so I ignored them again, and the same happened. I kept doing this while amassing more and more, until I had over a hundred, and then without anything being said, they erased the lot. They probably didn't want the idea catching on.

In my brothers' time, you'd be let off playing sports the week before your O Levels so you could revise, but this was another thing Jebb had changed. The day before our exams we'd been forced to play some particularly pointless "general games" cricket match. So Chris and I decided to put an early end to the game by asking everyone on our side to get themselves deliberately bowled out without scoring a single run.

Typically, one guy broke ranks and began scoring as many as he could. When it was my turn to go in, I waited until he was facing the bowler. He missed the shot, and the wicketkeeper picked it up. I then started charging towards his end. As it had gone behind him, it was my "call" whether or not run, so about a second before I got there, I shouted, "Run!"

I was safe, but he didn't have a chance. The wicketkeeper lobbed the ball to the bowler who tapped it against the bails. "Howzat!"

The next ball I 'accidentally' smashed my bat against the stumps and then walked off triumphant.

I wanted to make a big gesture before leaving. One of my brothers told me of a guy who'd performed some naked dance at an end-of-term film screening. It still made him laugh years later, so I decided I'd go one better and run naked (barring a jumper over my head) from our dormitory through the main hall into the dining room where half the school was eating Sunday dinner and back.

The teacher who was supervising gave chase, but I outran him and made it back to the dorm and quickly got dressed with only one guy seeing me. For a couple of days everyone was trying to guess who the streaker was, while I played dumb. Unfortunately, the guy who saw me changing was the Headboy's fag, and he must have blabbed as I then got a message saying Jebb wanted to see me. I ended up getting a ten quid fine, which I was able to raise with donations.

But my proudest achievement was what I called "the Abolish The School Song Campaign." This was a hymn in Latin and about the most tuneless dirge you could imagine - after three years I could barely hum it. Nevertheless, every few months whoever was leading Mass would announce, "...and today it's the School Song, hymn number 94!" like it was some big treat.

For several weeks I'd got a couple of friends to get everyone around us to pass their hymn books and tear out the offending page.

At last, the moment came - "And today it's the School Song, hymn number 94..." and we all started shaking with laughter as about half the school turned to each other in bemusement, followed by the most pathetic rendition ever given.

A couple of weeks later I finally said good riddance to that hell hole - though to this day I have a recurring dream I have to return to finish those last two years.

KELLY

Tues 17 Oct 2006

I ran into Grub Smith today, the guy I mentioned in the 'How to Pick Up Girls Pt. 2' essay who wrote the 'Laboratory of Love' column for FHM and got me and Raife into the 'sex' parties. He asked after Kelly, a porn model/stripper/hooker I once introduced him to because I thought they'd get on.

 I first saw her at the HQ club, where I met Christina, and she had a similar effect - picture a Baywatch-era Pamela Anderson with even bigger implants. I was so busy staring I didn't notice she was sitting next to a woman I knew called Simone who was waving for me to join them.

 After about an hour they said they were going on somewhere, and Kelly asked if we had any gigs coming up. I gave her a flier for one at The Garage in Islington, thinking I'd never see her again, but the two of them showed up a couple of songs from the end of our set and then started gyrating away at the front of the stage. Kelly was in a completely transparent top apart from an embroidered flower partly covering each nipple, and we were playing a '70s-ish funky wah-wah track called 'For Your Eyes', so it was quite a sight. Raife spent most of the song laughing.

 Though it wasn't her fault, it was because of what happened after that our original bassist Paul ended up leaving the band. There was an after-party, and I'd somehow ended up with both women on my arms. I literally had people shaking my hand and congratulating me. Sure enough, Kelly suggested we get a cab to Simone's, and just as we were getting into one, Paul appeared. "I hope you don't mind if I join you?" he said, and before anyone could think what to say, he pulled the door shut and the driver set off. Needless to say, the night was a write-off and there was no threesome.

A few days later we had another gig at The Garage ("The Upstairs" section this time). We'd just set up the gear when our roadie asked how my night had gone. Paul hadn't shown up yet, so I told him the story. He immediately began shaking his head and said that Paul had told him earlier he was going to make a move on Simone, adding, "I know it will fuck off Tim, but I don't care."

He'd dumped me in it on a number of occasions, but this was the first time I knew for sure he'd done it knowingly. By the time he arrived, I was fuming, and when he asked if I was okay, I let him have it. We played the gig without speaking, and a couple of days later he said he was leaving, and I said it was probably a good idea. (There were a load of other issues going on - musical and personal - so I doubt we'd have lasted much longer.)

Kelly and I eventually started going out, and I learned her life story, one of the most interesting I've ever heard.

At 16 she nearly died on the operating table and then married the doctor who'd saved her life. She was studying to be a doctor herself, but had to give it up when she became pregnant. At 24 she discovered her husband had been having an affair and took revenge by working behind his back in a strip club. This led to becoming an escort/hooker (prior to the affair, her husband was the only man she'd ever slept with). Whenever she discovered evidence he'd been unfaithful, she'd book herself into the local brothel and sleep with up to 30 men per shift. Eventually they divorced, and she had two more husbands while continuing to work as a porn actress/model - becoming a Penthouse Pet as well as making a "Top Ten Strippers in the US" list.

At various times she also had her own phone-in radio sex show, sang on a couple of minor charts hits and performed stand-up comedy in New York.

Every time I saw her, she'd come out with some amazing story I'd never heard before. One of my favourites was when she was shooting a gang-bang scene in a cornfield. There was a cropduster spraying a nearby field, and she said if you watch the film, you can hear the buzzing of the plane as the pilot kept circling and diving down to get a closer look.

By the time I introduced her to Grub, it was starting to die down between us, so I didn't mind when they started "seeing" each other. It so happened I'd had a fling with another hooker/porn model called Natalie who Grub also knew.

For his final 'Laboratory of Love' column, he'd booked four hookers, each from a different continent, plus a load of cocaine. It obviously got to him, as despite having all of them naked in his shower, he couldn't get it up. Still, a fitting end to such a career.

A VERY MAD WEEK

Wed 18 Oct 2006

By the time we got our eviction notice at Moravian, we were one of half a dozen remaining squats and about the same number of legitimate student flats in a block that once held over 50.

In a concerted effort to finally clear the place, the college/council had somehow arranged for our court dates to fall on the same day which was also when the last student tenancies were due to expire. To make sure none of the students sold on their keys (as had been happening), they'd also issued a warning that anyone caught doing so would forfeit their degrees. It didn't sound enforceable, but no one seemed willing to risk it.

The squatters who'd already moved out had either found places to rent or gone to more squat-friendly boroughs in the South or East. I didn't fancy reliving my Old Kent Road experience, so along with Julie and about five others also keen to maintain our upmarket squatting style we began scouring the area for places with potential.

There weren't many council-owned properties in Kensington and Chelsea as it was, let alone empty ones. Jim and Paul broke into a couple of derelict private places, but they were just too far gone with things like missing flooring or holes in the roof.

A week before the court date Julie and I were leaving Moravian to do our daily squat hunt when we ran into one of the squatters who'd already moved out, a Mancunian guy called Mick. We asked if he happened to know any potential squats in the area, and to our surprise he did and went on to describe a four-storey block 'somewhere behind Sloane Square' that was about 50% squatted. It was another forced sell-off by the council, so the legal tenants were apparently sympathetic to the squatters, making for a really cool atmosphere. The previous summer they'd been holding big open parties in the courtyard with sound systems rigged to people's cars. He told us there were three flats currently empty (just enough to house us and our friends), but we should move quick before someone else took them.

We didn't need persuading, but when we asked for the address, he said, "You'll have to make it worth my while." This was about as far from squatting etiquette as it got (there'd been a particularly strong sense of camaraderie at Moravian), and we told him to forget it without even asking his price.

It wasn't just the principle. After he left, Julie and I realised we'd been thinking the same thing - he'd already given us enough information that we should be able to find it ourselves easily enough and headed towards Sloane Square in search of a four-storey council block with a courtyard/car park.

It wasn't until we got there that we realised how broadly one can interpret "behind" Sloane Square. We were also unaware how many estates were tucked away between there and Victoria (the next main tube station). By the time it was dark, we'd checked about four or five estates, but none matched the description.

The next day also yielded nothing, so we extended our search up towards Knightsbridge where we finally stumbled on a four-storey block with a courtyard/car park. We looked for signs of vacancy (no curtains, bare light bulbs) and saw two flats that looked definitely empty and another possible one.

We still weren't sure if it was the right block, though, or if it was even council-owned. Although there were a couple of washing lines across the balconies, there were no screaming kids or blaring radios that you normally got in council or even housing trust blocks. The tenants we saw (mostly women, for some reason) also didn't look particularly rich - which they'd had to have been to live in the area if it was privately owned. It was hard to put a finger on, but there was something odd about the place that we both felt.

We went back to Moravian and explained the situation to Jim. We didn't want to risk losing the flats, so he suggested the two of us go over the next day, secure a couple and then try to find out who owned the block. It might still be possible to stay even if they were private/housing trust.

As soon as we got there, Jim understood what we meant about the atmosphere – it just seemed a little too well-behaved. We decided to stick to the plan, though, and got the door open on the first flat on our list. Although it was empty, there was some builder's equipment inside, meaning a swift PIO order (person in occupation) if we tried to move in. We pulled the door shut and then went to the second flat on our list. That was properly vacant, so we changed the lock and then went to the last one. It was also empty, although there was no electricity. We opened the mains box where there was one empty terminal and a big hanging wire. We shoved it in and a light came on.

We spent the night in that one and the next morning went to a call box and rang the council to ask if they owned it. No one seemed to know, so we went back to the flat to figure out our next move. We then got a knock from Kieron, one our Moravian friends, who'd been given the address by Julie. He said he'd passed the caretaker's flat just down the road who would obviously know who owned it and offered to pay him a visit.

Jim and I spent the next 20 minutes going, "Please, God, let it be council," while wondering what was taking Kieron so long.

Finally, we saw him sauntering up the road with a big smile. Assuming this meant good news, Jim shouted down, "So it's council, yeah?"

Kieron shook his head, but continued grinning.

"So what then? Housing trust?"

"I'll explain when I get up!" he shouted back, almost laughing now.

He was in the same boat as us, so it was all very odd. We were so desperate to find out what was going on, we decided to take the lift to meet him. Just as we got in, a couple of officious-looking characters joined us. One asked what we were doing in the building, so I said we lived there.

"Oh, really? And how is that exactly?"

"Er, well, we're actually squatting."

He pulled out his police ID and said we were under arrest.

They took us to the station and then put us in separate cells. When I asked for a lawyer, they said none were available until the next day. They also wouldn't let me make a phone call. After a couple of hours, one of them said I'd be free to leave if I agreed to a short interview. Jim and I knew to use the standard squatters' defence if were caught (that we'd found the flats open and then changed the locks), so I figured it would be safe. The first question was if I knew who owned the place. Funny you should ask...

It turned out that the block where we'd broken into three flats in broad daylight, was affordable housing for the borough's police force and their families.

Suddenly everything began making sense - the strange Stepford Wives-like atmosphere, Kieron's big smile and why they were trying to deny us a lawyer, phonecall, etc. Not exactly good publicity for them if it got out squatters had moved in.

Then one of them told me a drill had gone missing from the first place we'd broken into (with the builder's equipment inside) and they'd have to search the other two flats before they'd let us go. It sounded unlikely, but I knew we didn't have it, so I said okay. Jim had been given the same treatment and also agreed to the search. They drove us back over, and one cop took Jim to the second flat while I was taken to the third where we'd spent the night.

Just as we were entering, the cop escorting me said, "I hope you didn't switch on the power, by the way, because then we'd have to do you for theft."

Instead of checking the mains box, he then went to the living room where there was a double light switch, each controlling a different bulb. I knew only one of them worked, and he happened to hit the one that didn't.

"You were lucky there," he said - not realising how lucky.

After a cursory search, we were taken back to the station and then told we had to sign a final statement renouncing any claim to the flats. I knew we could have refused, but we just wanted to get the hell out by this point.

We now had just three days to leave Moravian. While the others started searching further afield, Julie and I continued looking for the original block Mick told us about.

The next day we took a different route back and passed a four-storey block opposite Chelsea Army barracks where someone had spray-painted a "CND" symbol and knew instantly we'd found it. As we walked in, a couple of ex-Moravian guys said hello to us and then showed us the flats which were still empty.

Jim and I got them all open that evening, and with less than 24 hours before our eviction, we'd all moved into our new address at Cheylesmore House, SW1 (just down from Buckingham Palace Road).

The next morning Julie and I went to pick up some last bits from Moravian. I saw one of the students moving some boxes from his first floor flat, and we got chatting about it being the end of an era. A few of us had been saying that if we could just keep one squat open, the council wouldn't be able to close the front off as they were planning and then others might be able to move in and keep the party going for a while longer. On the off-chance, I asked if he'd sell us his keys for £20, and he agreed on the condition I didn't tell the college.

So about an hour before the bailiffs were due, Julie and I moved into the flat (the only flat with its own balcony) and anxiously waited for the knock. (In the meantime, the student got nervous and returned the money - though he let us keep the keys.)

Almost on the dot, there was a shout through the letterbox that the bailiff was about to seal the front and for anyone inside to leave immediately. I shouted back that we were legally squatting it. After a short silence, he shouted back he'd be closing it anyway.

Stupidly, I decided to go outside to try to reason with him. As soon as I opened the door, he came charging at me. I managed to push him back and told Julie to lock the door while I went to call the police - who legally would be obliged to prevent the bailiff entering.

The only working phone was busy, and by the time I got back, the bailiff had called the cops himself. One of them asked how we'd got into the flat. Not wanting to break my promise, I told him I'd climbed up from the street onto the balcony, found the back door open and then changed the front lock from the inside.

"That's quite a high balcony," he said, "Do you mind showing me how you did it?"

We went back out onto the street, and it was higher than I realised, so I told him I'd been given a leg up. "Show me," he said, clasping his hands together. I then found myself in the bizarre situation of climbing onto this cop's shoulders on the King's Road and us then both toppling over.

I'd managed to touch the railings, though, and he said I'd shown it was possible. We went back to the flat, where his partner had been examining the door frame and saw there was dry paint on it, the same colour as on the lock - proving I hadn't just changed it, as I'd claimed. So close.

A few hours later a massive steel plate was put over the entrance, and that was the end of Moravian as we knew it, as well as a very mad week.

PREDICTING MUSIC FASHIONS

Thurs 19 Oct 2006

Toby and I went to The Arts Club again last night. He mentioned earlier he'd be doing a short DJ set. I asked what kind of music he played, and he said it was mainly the same '60s and '70s acts I'm into, though he liked to slip in a few '80s tracks when he could. I asked if there were any in particular he liked, expecting it to be indie-type stuff or people like New Order and The Smiths, but instead he started talking about Bruce Springsteen, Kylie Minogue and even Belinda Carlisle - whose 'Heaven Is a Place on Earth' he described as "classic pop."

At the club I got chatting to a guy called Jim Jones who I've known since the '90s when he fronted a very Stooges/Stones-y band called Thee Hypnotics. He now sings for Black Moses and introduced me to their new drummer, Simon. They were both complaining about the glut of '80s tracks the DJ was playing (not Toby) as well as the '80s revival in general that's very big right now with acts like Scissor Sisters, Franz Ferdinand, the Darkness, etc., plus clubs like Trash, Plastic People and the whole 'electroclash' scene. A band then came on who Jim described as "a bad Gang of Four" - another '80s act he said everyone has been ripping off lately.

As someone who lived through that time, I did not see this coming. In fact, if there was one decade I was convinced no one would ever revive, except as part of some bad taste theme night, it was that one. But I have to concede these people genuinely seem to like this stuff and it's not some 'so bad, it's good'-irony thing.

The first time I heard anyone talk about the '80s with affection was Kim, who told me she and her friends had gone through a big Spandau Ballet phase while studying for their A Levels. She also said it was her favourite decade for both fashion and film and that she felt there was something "magical" about that time. This caught my attention as it's exactly how I feel about the '60s.

I'd already noticed, people often seem to feel an affinity for the time around their birth, including myself (I was born in the mid '60s). I then realised Kim and her friends would also all have been born when this music was being made.

The best explanation I've come up with for this is that while in the womb or the first year or two of life, we're in a particularly receptive psychic state and pick up some of the mood of that time which we later associate with the contented state we were in back then - a kind of 'womb nostalgia'. I realise this falls a little outside conventional scientific thinking.

As the '80s revival grew, I noticed almost everyone involved was around the same age as Kim, so would also have been born when it was being made. (Toby is also that age.) I then realised that every main revival occurred about 20 years after the period being revived (*see table below for examples)*, which, if there's anything to my theory, could be because this is when you have enough like-minded people simultaneously reaching club or gig-going age to form the basis of a scene.

I hadn't really contributed to the anti-'80s conversation, but at some point Jim had to leave, so I told my theory to Simon who seemed very taken with it. He said he was born in 1973 when most of his favourite music was made, including his favourite album of all time (by the Stooges) which he said sounded more modern to him than anything current (again, this is how I feel about my two favourite albums, *Rubber Soul* and *Revolver*). He then started talking about other people he knew who were obsessed with the period around the time they were born.

We discussed less "esoteric" explanations. The most obvious is that we were simply exposed to this music when very young, but there was barely any music in our house when I grew up, and he said it was the same for him. It could also be to do with what you hear in your early teens or when first getting into music. Though I'm sure that can be a big factor, Simon said he didn't get into the Stooges until he was older, and while I did hear a lot of '60s stuff in my early teens, I don't feel a particular affinity for the current music from that time (and which I was also being exposed to).

After coming up with my 'womb nostalgia'/revivals-come-20-years-later theory, I identified two other mechanisms governing fashions in music and drew up a theory linking them all as a way of predicting the next major change and its likely nature - with potential applications for the fashion industry and particularly clueless A and R men.

I mentioned this to Simon, who then told me he actually lectures on rock culture (!) and that if I gave him an outline of the full theory, he could probably get me work delivering it as a talk to various colleges (he said it pays well). I'm not sure how I feel about this, but I said I'd send it. For anyone interested, this is the whole thing.

1. SEVEN-YEAR ITCH

This concerns the really big shifts in fashion. I've heard it said that a sea-change occurs every ten years, but if one takes 1955 as rock's "Year Zero," it's clear the cycles are closer to every seven years, thus:

1955 - 'Rock Around the Clock' reaches Number 1. Also first big hits for Elvis, Jerry Lee Lewis, Chuck Berry, etc.

1963 - Beatles' first No 1.

1970 - Beatles split. Also deaths of Jimi Hendrix, Brian Jones, Janis Joplin, followed by the simultaneous emergence of heavy rock (Led Zep, Black Sabbath, etc.) and the singer/songwriter movement (Neil Young, James Taylor, Joni Mitchell, etc.).

1977 - Punk/new wave.

1983 - New romantic movement plus synth-pop (Soft Cell, Gary Numan, Human League, etc.).

1990 - 'Madchester'/rave scene in the UK. Emergence of Seattle/grunge scene in the US.

1996/7 - Britpop (Pulp, Elastica, Blur, etc.).

2004/5 - Current '80s revival/electroclash, etc.

Fashions may also be triggered by an external factor such as the introduction of a new instrument or effect (e.g., wah pedals at the end of the '60s, samplers in the mid '80s) or a new drug becoming popular (e.g., amphetamines leading to mod, LSD leading to psychedelia, ecstasy leading to rave culture). This can occur at any time, but tends to result in shorter lived scenes.

2. PENDULUM EFFECT

This concerns the nature of the fashion shifts which are usually a reaction to the one that preceded it (e.g., the 'back to basics'/stripped-down approach that followed psychedelia around 1968 with *Music From The Big Pink*, *The Basement Tapes*, *Beggars Banquet*, *The White Album,* etc., or the street style and minimalism of punk that followed the bloated excesses of prog rock - and was then itself replaced by escapism and aspirations to glamour of the New Romantics).

3. REVIVALS

(As previously mentioned) these usually occur around 20 years after the period being revived, thus:

The '50s revival of the mid '70s (Mud, Showaddywaddy, Alvin Stardust, etc. Also, TV shows and films such as *Happy Days*, *American Graffiti* and *That'll Be The Day* all set during that period).

The '60s/psychedelic revival of the mid/late '80s (Green On Red, Dream Syndicate, REM, 'Paisley Underground' scene).

The influence of early '70s music (Led Zep, Black Sabbath, Neil Young, etc.) on the Seattle/'grunge' scene in the early '90s.

The influence of punk/new wave on the Britpop scene circa 1997/8.

The current '80s revival.

As when planets align in astrology, cycles sometimes overlap, reinforcing their effect. This happened when ecstasy became popular just as a seven-year shift was due around 1990, resulting in the Madchester/acid house scene. The same happened around 1997 when a seven-year shift coincided with the due punk/new wave revival, leading to Britpop.

We are currently witnessing a rare conjunction of all three, with the seven-year shift occurring at the same time as the due '80s revival, which is the natural reaction, musically and image-wise, to bands like Oasis, Travis, Keen, etc., who previously dominated. This is why the movement is much bigger than by all rights it should have been. That's my explanation, and I'm sticking to it.

Now the more obvious extremes have been covered and the internet has dissipated fashions into ever smaller niches, I'm not sure how long these forces will continue to apply, but it may still be worth buying stocks of old "Smiley" t-shirts for the expected acid house revival due around 2012.

After the Gang Of Four-alikes came off stage, Toby began his DJ set, and the first track he played was 'Drive My Car', recorded (it so happens) the day I was born. There's not many tracks that compel me to dance, but that's one of them, and I left Simon to make an idiot of myself.

MADNESS ATTRACTS MADNESS

Fri 20 Oct 2006

If you really want to know me, you need to know about the Italian girl. I met her on a New Year's Eve at the Lonsdale pub on Portobello Road a few years back. We had a very dirty night and spent every day of the next couple of weeks together, when she finally had to return home.

About a month later she came back here, and we picked things up where we'd left them, and she then decided to move here permanently.

Though only around 20, she seemed to have an endless supply of hilarious stories, like the time she kickboxed some guy who'd been following her down a flight of steps or the ex-boyfriend whose flat she destroyed with a baseball bat because he wouldn't stop calling.

In retrospect, these should have rung alarm bells, but at the time all I thought was, 'finally a girl with attitude, who lives by her own rules'.

The first time I personally witnessed something that gave me cause for concern was back at the Lonsdale one night. I was talking to some friends when she said she had to go outside. I went to check on her and found her in the road in a kind of daze. When I asked if she was okay, it was as if she couldn't even see me.

I got her home and she gradually returned to normal. She said she'd had similar episodes in the past, but they seemed to be happening more frequently.

A couple of weeks later we were coming back to mine via Holland Park Avenue and I mentioned my boots were starting to rub.

"You need to break them in," she said.

The boots were quite old and hadn't rubbed before, so I said it was more likely the skin on my feet had softened from not having worn them for a while.

"No," she said, "It's the boots. They need breaking in."

"But I've had them for years," I replied, "and they didn't used to rub. I think I just need to rebuild the callouses."

"No. You need to break them in."

"But I already said. They're old boots, and they were okay before."

"You need to wear them in."

The conversation went on like this for at least 20 minutes - her saying they needed breaking in and me saying they were old and used to be fine.

The boots weren't the real issue - at least in my mind. It was the fact she wasn't even acknowledging my point, but when I told her this, she said it was the other way around and I was the one refusing to listen.

We ended up laughing about it all, and I remember telling a friend we'd had our first argument, but at least it wasn't over anything serious.

A few weeks later I helped find her a flat, and as thanks she invited me for a dinner. As she was preparing the food, I mentioned I'd been invited to dinner a couple of days before by some Maltese girl I knew. I was looking to get out of it, but before I got to that part, she turned to me coldly and said, "You've fucked this girl, haven't you?" I hadn't and said so.

"You have really, though, haven't you?"

"Honestly, no. She's not even my type. I was actually looking for an excuse to..."

"I don't mind if you have. I'd just prefer if you told me the truth."

"But I'm telling you the truth."

"No, you're not. It's okay, though."

We'd been getting on well before, and at first I thought she was joking, but she kept going and getting more and more nasty.

"...I know you fucked her. I just wish you'd admit it, instead of treating me like some fucking idiot."

"But how can I admit it? I didn't fuck her!"

"I know you did."

The killer was when she said, "The more you deny it, the more I know it's true." What the hell do you say to that?

This went on for a good 25 minutes when I finally told her I'd had enough and was leaving. Right as I got to the door, she covered the handle.

"I'm sorry. I believe you now. Please don't go."

"Really?"

"Yes. I just had to be sure."

We went back to joking around until about ten minutes later when her voice turned hard again. "You did fuck her really, though, didn't you?"

She dropped it eventually and spent the next few days apologising and saying she didn't know what came over her.

A few weeks later I got a call from the police saying to come to her neighbours' flat. When I got there, her face was streaked with mascara and she was shaking so much she could barely talk. The cops explained they'd been called out after she'd screamed from her window there were intruders inside and later told them they'd been in there for three hours while she'd been hiding behind her door with a hot iron in case they came in.

But what was actually more scary was that they'd found no evidence anyone had even been in the flat. Nothing had been moved, and the locks were untouched. There were also no footprints in the flowerbed outside (where she said they'd run out after she began screaming), and none of the neighbours had heard or seen anything either.

About a month later she sounded very odd on the phone. I asked what was up, and she said she was thinking of going back that night to Italy "...Either that or I might set fire to myself. I haven't decided yet."

I raced over, and she had the same dazed look she'd had outside the Lonsdale, while the flat looked like a bomb had gone off, with papers and clothes strewn everywhere. I sat with her until the early morning when her mood finally began to lift.

There were a couple more incidents like that, and the arguments were also becoming more frequent. A few times I said I'd had enough, or else she'd tell me to leave, but as soon as I got home, the phone calls would start with her pleading to give it another go until I'd finally relent.

The obvious question is, why did I keep going back? Some of it was concern. I was one of the only people she knew here, and I was afraid she would end up in a ward or going full *Betty Blue* (her favourite film). But the bigger reason was that somewhere along the line I fell in love.

I know how that sounds, but I've mostly talked about the fucked-up stuff and her bad side. When she wasn't freaking out, she was as sane as anyone - more so in many ways - and her good side was as loving and kind as the bad side was horrible.

She was as open as a kid, smothering me in kisses when I walked in the door, and would hide notes in the books I was reading saying I was the only person she'd ever loved and thanking me for putting up with her.

Normally I'd start climbing the walls if I spent more than a couple of days in a row with someone, but with her it was impossible to be bored. Even a visit to the shop would somehow turn into an adventure or like an (early) scene from *Betty Blue*. She was also extremely funny and could have me hurting with laughter. If I was down about something, she'd put on a sad expression and go, "Tweety Pie!" in this ludicrous, moronic voice until I could no longer keep a straight face.

I haven't even mentioned how she looked - as beautiful as any girl I'd seen and seemed to look more beautiful each day. The sex was also like nothing I'd experienced. Just touching felt like an electrical charge. We'd get up to all kinds of dirty stuff, while at other times it was so tender, it was almost mystical.

I'd finally found someone I was completely crazy about, who felt the same way about me. We had the important stuff. If there was just some way to stop the freak-outs and arguments, it would be perfect.

She said they were based on a fear of being abandoned, and we'd talk for hours about how to avoid them. She'd be completely lucid when talking like this, saying how she really needed to sort herself out and that all she wanted was to make things work. So I'd be thinking, *Okay, she gets it and she wants to change - there's hope.* But none of it made any difference. In fact, the arguments got worse.

They could come out of anywhere, and almost anything could set them off - asking where she'd put the butter or arriving a few minutes later than I'd said (though she'd routinely keep me waiting a couple of hours). Once she suggested spending the whole of the next day together. I said I'd need half an hour to finish a song we were due to record. That was enough to send her into a rage lasting the entire night. Eventually, she fell asleep - only to start screaming at me the moment she woke up.

I'd tell her I loved her or whatever else she'd suggested I should do in her saner moments, but if I referred to anything she'd said, then she'd scream, "I only said that stuff because you made me," or accuse me of trying to control her, her face contorted in anger.

She'd sometimes refer to the freak-outs as her "Monster," and the switch was so fast and dramatic, I began to wonder if maybe there was some malevolent entity involved. We'd be laughing and joking one minute, and literally the next she'd start accusing me of something I hadn't done or spitting insults ("You're fucked up; your whole family is fucked up") over and over, as if goading me into a fight. At times it was like "It" could read my mind, homing in on some personal insecurity I didn't even know I had - until eventually I'd lose it myself, and then all hell would break loose.

Sometimes instead of yelling, she'd turn to me and go, "You see, this just proves we're not compatible," and then coldly announce it was over. It could have been over something as trivial as not liking (or not hating) the same TV presenter. I'd then have to spend hours trying to convince her it wasn't worth breaking up over until it felt like my head would explode.

I'd try to avoid the scenes by saying I was going home, but then she began threatening that if I did, she'd go onto the street and ask a stranger to have sex. She'd done similar stuff before we'd met, so I knew she was capable, and that it really would be the end if she did such was my growing jealousy. So it was like there was no escape.

Some of the scenes were pure insanity. One New Year's Eve she suggested watching a porn film and then freaked out because she thought I was staring at one of the girls too much! I then had to physically hold her down to prevent her running naked apart from a fur coat onto Portobello Road packed with drunken revellers. Another time after crying and screaming for several hours she dived head first and fully clothed into an empty bath and then turned the shower on herself.

And as fast as she'd lost it, she could switch back. A few minutes after diving into the bath, she said quietly, "I'm so sorry. I've been a nightmare." The softness returned to her face, and she spent the rest of the night apologising and asking how she could make it up to me - as if having inflicted maximum damage, the Monster decided its job was done, leaving us to pick up the pieces.

We'd become one of those awful couples you see screaming at each other on the street and the next time they're all over each other. I used to looked at people like that and think, "You're obviously terrible for each other - just end it!" Now I understood why they didn't, because with some people it really is an addiction.

Numerous times I swore I'd had enough and was never going back, but after a couple of days, it was like this physical craving would kick in and I couldn't think of anything else. The sexual temptation was the hardest to resist, plus she'd be feeling the same and calling every couple of hours.

"I know we can't be together, but can't we at least have sex?"
"It's too risky. We'll just slip back into it."
"But I don't want that either. Come on, I really need to fuck. It doesn't have to mean anything."
"I'm not sure."
"Just this once? For old times' sake?"
Two junkies talking themselves into a final fix before they quit.
"Okay, but only sex. Nothing else."

As soon as we touched, the cravings would begin to ease and the sex would be even more intense for the time spent apart. Afterwards, we'd be like magnets with neither wanting the other to leave. For a couple of days it was like heaven, then just as I was starting to relax, the icey look would come into her eye and I knew the Monster was back.

It wasn't just the arguments causing problems. Because of her temperament, she'd regularly get fired from jobs or kicked out of flats, so she'd be lurching from one crisis to the next and constantly panicking that she was one step away from the streets. This was also happening as we were putting out our first album, so I'd often be coming to a session or photo shoot completely shattered after some all-night screaming match.

What I've talked about is honestly about 1% of the shit that happened, and I haven't even mentioned the time she was taken off a plane on a drip after swallowing a bag of speed to get through the flight, the French girl she invited to move in despite knowing she'd once held her boyfriend up at knife-point for three hours and who later threatened to have me killed, the guy she kickboxed on Golborne Road after he nearly drove into us, who then knocked me unconscious with a rolling pin he'd grabbed from a stall, and then on the same street, the same week, the gang of Moroccans who surrounded me after she screamed they all needed psychotherapy.

I couldn't help noticing a tragicomic element to how I seemed to always be paying the price for the trouble she caused, and when I wasn't thinking of demonic entities, I'd see myself as part of this game show for the gods and imagine them roaring with laughter as they watched my latest exploits.

For a couple of years I more or less handled it, but the stress gradually got to me. My weight dropped to 8 ½ stone (I'm 5ft 11), and I could feel myself losing it mentally, until I finally made the break.

I'd still run into her from time to time, and she'd either be really nice or treat me like a virtual stranger. Once she asked how I'd been, and I mentioned that a couple of days before I was hit and nearly run over by a bus (did I mention tragicomic?). She just said, "Oh," and then said she had to go somewhere. I'd seen her be completely indifferent to people's pain before, but realising (at that moment at least) this person I'd loved with all my heart didn't care if I lived or died was like a knife through me.

I was already in a bad way, but I now spiralled into something worse than anything I'd been through. I began deliberately putting myself into dangerous situations, basically hoping something or someone would put an end to the pain. This was on top of a mountain of band and label problems which on their own could have brought me close to breakdown. (If you haven't already guessed, this was the really dark period I mentioned in the 'Aims, Ames and Amie' essay.) *See also 'MDH - the Early Years.'*

A few years later, I was reading a book on Keith Moon and started noticing some very similar traits - the uncontrolled rages lasting hours at a time (the hotel destroying wasn't just a show), the sudden switches to lucidity and self-awareness and also the loveable childlike side.

Towards the end, the author suggested he may have suffered from a condition called borderline personality disorder and listed the nine key traits - of which four or more held persistently is considered sufficient for a diagnosis. Like him, she had all nine.

I know I'm not a psychiatrist, but I saw this stuff up close, and some of the traits are very specific, such as dysphoria lasting a few hours, no consistent sense of "self," chronic fear of abandonment (real or imagined), "splitting" (alternating between ideation and hatred), etc. The name makes it sound like a mild condition, but it's considered one of the most serious (around 10% commit suicide) and notoriously difficult to treat - though some do apparently recover.

I know someone who worked in a psychiatric hospital in Bermuda. He told a funny story of a woman who believed she was the cause of various wars and disasters. As she was telling him this, a TV was showing some Apollo rocket launch which suddenly exploded. "See?" she said and carried on talking. He said odd stuff like that seemed to happen a lot with such people, as if they somehow attracted it. I'd noticed this myself. Although a lot of what occurred was due to her own actions, some very strange stuff happened that had nothing to do with her, and there's one more story I'd like to recount as it illustrates this point and how surreal my life felt back then.

For a long time we'd discussed having a threesome. We'd got close a few times, but something always went wrong. Then one time she had a friend from her home town come to stay, and on her last night they ended up kissing. Later the girl said she'd be up for a threesome, but we'd have to go there to do it.

As keen as I was, I wasn't prepared to travel 1,500 miles for one, but she kept saying how much fun it would be and it was a chance to see where she grew up, until I finally said yes.

As soon as we got there, we met the friend in a bar and they went for a private chat. Ten minutes later she came back. "It's not happening. She says there was a misunderstanding."

To console ourselves we tried to score some hash, but we'd apparently arrived during their worst dope drought in years.

The next day we arranged to meet a childhood friend of hers called Vicenzo who said he could get us some, but he never showed up.

The day after that was a Saturday, when she said there was some park where dealers always showed up at a certain time. Earlier we'd heard someone had been stabbed to death at a football match between Genova and AC Milan. Nothing like that had happened before in Italy, so everyone who was waiting in this park to score was talking about it.

Then some guy came running over and started talking fast in Italian. Suddenly all I heard was, "Putana Madonna!" and, "ma figurati" (I don't believe it).

I asked what was going on.

"The guy who got stabbed at the match - it was Vicenzo."

A couple of days later we went to the memorial service, and it was like a scene from The Godfather with people weeping and looking stunned. Players from both football teams were there, and people had come just to get their autographs, so it ended up this complete circus. A couple of TV crews were also filming, and someone told us later there was a close-up of us on Rai Uno, their main TV station, with her in a leopard skin coat crying on my shoulder. If that wasn't surreal enough, it was followed by a statement from the Pope in praise of the guy we'd tried scoring off a couple of days before. I remember thinking *I came here for a threesome. How the fuck did it turn into this?*

And that was only the first part of the holiday. It managed to go further downhill after that if you can believe it, but I think that's enough crazy stories for one day.

WEIRD SHIT HAPPENS

Sat 21 Oct 2006

Before talking to Simon about music fashions at the Arts Club the other night, I was chatting to a friend who knows I've been writing these essays and he asked how they were going. I said some weird stuff had been happening since starting them, but I didn't really go into it as it was loud where we were standing, plus I haven't got my head around it all myself. About as close as I've come are vague phrases I keep writing in my notebook, like "double-backing," "everything turning in on itself" and "life imitating art imitating life." But I'm going to talk about it now and see if I can make some sense of it.

I started these essays just after finishing *I Love You More Than You Know* by Jonathan Ames. Aside from some old stories and ideas I hoped to include somewhere, I didn't really know what I'd be writing about or how it would all turn out.

Sometimes I'd choose one of these old stories or ideas, but I soon discovered that unless I felt genuinely in the mood to write about them, they'd invariably come out dry or forced and I'd end up giving up. As I had to write something each day, I'd usually end up just talking about whatever was uppermost on my mind and basically ramble away until I'd run out of anything to say. I'd then be left with a jumble of stuff, with a few bits I liked, so I'd start cutting the irrelevant boring bits, move some things around and clean up the phrasing until out of the mess an essay would emerge.

This is very similar to the "spill out everything, clean up and polish" process I talked about in the essay on songwriting ('Who

Writes The Songs?'), and there can be a similar sense of surprise at how the various strands end up coming together or resolving into some neat conclusion I might not have intended or even thought about when I began it.

Usually at some point I'd feel properly in the mood to write about whatever subject I'd given up on, and not only would I enjoy writing it, but it would also read much better - fitting with the main point of 'Who Writes The Songs?' about the importance of having fun to the creative process.

It took a while for me to notice these parallels as the songwriting essay was itself a product of the "spill out everything" process, and it was only through writing it that I came to this conclusion. But the more I've thought about it, the more I decided I'd stumbled on an important truth and I've increasingly made it a "rule" only to write what I feel most in the mood to talk about on any particular day - leaving me with the strange feeling of being taught about creativity by what I myself wrote on the subject.

Sometimes when I returned to an essay I'd abandoned, I'd have written something in the interim that I might refer to or expand on.

This happened with the Beatles essay which I'd begun a few days before, but wasn't enjoying. By the time I was in the mood, I'd written the essay on Holmewood (where I discovered them). By mentioning this, I had a better introduction to the one I'd had as well as an angle (why people become so obsessed with them), improving both the essay and the overal flow of essays and which I wouldn't have been able to do had I finished it when I wasn't in the mood.

A few times a random incident or meeting would put me in the mood to write about one of the stories or subjects I'd wanted to include from the start or one I'd started and abandoned, and again I'd often incorporate it into the essay, helping to make it less "dry." An example of this was my '5 Categories Of Love' theory which

I'd tried to shoe-horn into an earlier essay, but ended up removing as it felt forced. But when it happened to come up when talking to Lou after she came back to mine on my birthday, I was able to mention it within the context of everything else that happened that night, providing a natural framework, and with the misunderstanding over her question ("So where are we then?") - an ending.

A similar thing happened with my 'Predicting Music Fashions' theory which I'd also tried writing before, but gave up on. But when it came up naturally while talking to Simon at the Arts Club, I was able to include it along with the events leading up to it and then tie it all together due to Toby happening to start DJing with 'Drive My Car', recorded the day I was born.

But where things start getting odd is how these random incidents and meetings would often not just put me in the mood to write about something I'd wanted to include from the start, but occurring when they did would also allow me to expand on or refer to something I'd written about in the interim – improving both the essay and overall sequence of essays – and which I wouldn't have been able to do had I completed them when I wasn't in the mood, forcing me to question how 'random' they really are.

An example of this was when I recently ran into Grub Smith and he asked if I'd seen Kelly. I'd wanted to write about her from the start, but couldn't find an "excuse." But this allowed me to talk about both her and Natalie (who I'd also wanted to mention) as she was one of the four hookers Grub hired for his final 'Laboratory of Love' column which I'd previously talked about in 'How to Pick Up Girls Pt. 2'. So I was able to refer back to that and tie it all together with how he couldn't get it up and how this was a fitting ending to such a career.

To some extent these apparently random, but perfectly timed, events have been happening from the start, e.g., when Kim rang to invite me to her party – giving me the opportunity to write about our relationship and expand on what I'd written in the very first essay about men and women and which I was able to further develop in the next day's essay about Gi (who I'd also wanted to write about), thanks to her email asking if she could rent her old room, etc., etc.

The net result is that instead of this just being a collection of unconnected stories, theories, etc., as I originally expected, it's morphed into this elaborate part-diary, part-biography, part-philosophy thing with various recurring characters and themes and this backwards/forwards timeline - such that I'm starting to worry people will think I had it all mapped out from the start, when all I've really been doing on both the macro and micro level is winging it.

Having written so much about the past, it's made me aware that I've been through a few pretty difficult periods in my life. A lot of things haven't worked out how I'd hoped, and in many ways it would have been better if I'd never moved to London or even tried getting into music. But I can honestly say it's a decision I've not regretted for a single second.

Even the difficult times feel like necessary stages I had to go through to teach me things that would prove important later. For example, if it hadn't been for my bad early landlord experiences and terrifying night on the Old Kent Road, I probably wouldn't have ended up squatting on the Kings Road, which was an amazing experience. Or if I hadn't been kicked out of Chelsea, I may not have decided to form my own band based around my own songs.

This reminded me of what I said in 'How to Pick Up Girls Pt. 2' about how you never regret following your instinct/intuition (which I believe I was doing by moving to London) and that even if you don't know why you feel compelled to do certain things, eventually "the wisdom becomes apparent."

I have to say I felt a bit uneasy about that section as I haven't always followed my instincts and I'm not even certain if it's true or that you can apply them to literally anything as I said. But that part came out in a strong burst, and when I tried to remove, it kept coming back into my head, so I ended up leaving it in.

I've had this a lot while writing, where a phrase or idea comes into my head almost fully formed, and if I try to remove it, it keeps returning as if my subconscious, Higher Self or whatever is behind the creative process won't allow me.

Sometimes a phrase or idea comes into my head, but I can't seem to find any place for it. It's like having an almost-completed jigsaw with a leftover piece that doesn't seem to go anywhere. I can't seem to relax or even just watch some TV without hearing all the sections going round in my head in different orders, trying to find some place for it and finally solve the puzzle. This is when creativity turns from fun to plain hard work (another common part of the process).

It's actually worse than I'm describing, because I never know for sure if there is a way to make it work - until at some point it hits me that something I'd assumed was okay actually wasn't. A section near the end should come earlier, for example. So I move that and then realise the bit I had leftover will fit between that and the section before. Suddenly the pieces start locking together and I get to see what my subconscious, Higher Self, etc., wanted to say and why it wouldn't let me relax until I'd achieved it.

Something else I've noticed from writing so much about the past is how a lot of the stories read like fiction, with a natural beginning, middle and end, often including a "lesson" or "moral" of some kind or hingeing on some amazing coincidence.

I even noticed this with the essay on Holmewood and the Dickens-like way the teachers' names seemed to subtley match their characters (Mr Dear, Quick, Burdon, Mrs Christie etc.). Admittedly, they only read this way after they'd been through the cutting and polishing process, though even here I'd often find myself working more by intuition/instinct rather than logic, with certain phrases or ideas coming into my head fully formed or "feeling" like they needed to be moved or cut.

Some of the most "meaningful" stuff and oddest coincidences seemed to happen when looking for places to live or trying to pull, when I was maybe relying more on my instincts. This made me think of what I wrote in the 'Hatcham Social' essay about how when acting on hunches "life takes on a fiction or movie-like feel." I'd never thought of it in those terms before, but that was another part that came into my head and which I couldn't remove without it feeling wrong.

This made me wonder if these events were inherently "meaningful" or "fiction-like" or if by choosing to write about something, my subconcious, Higher Self or whatever starts looking for the "meaning" or story and then nags at me to tell it in a certain way.

Given I seem incapable of completing an essay unless feeling genuinely in the mood, I'm not sure I can say I've "chosen" to write any of them, but as the fiction-like thing also applies to things I had no influence on like the teachers' names at Holmewood, that doesn't fully explain it either. It's a bit like one of those unanswerable "what is the sound of one hand clapping?" Buddhist koans that are meant to put you into a Zen trance just by contemplating them.

But as I said, I haven't always followed my instincts. As messed up as things became with my Italian ex, I think I followed them initially. If I'd left early on, I'd probably have spent my whole life wondering if I could have made it work, or she might have followed through on her fire threats, in which case I'd probably never have forgiven myself.

But there was a point about six months from the end where I

knew it was doomed and no longer feared she'd do something stupid. The reason I didn't leave then was because I couldn't bear the thought of her being with someone else and was trying to avoid the inevitable. Had I left when my instincts were telling me, I think I'd have recovered much sooner as I'd still have had some self-respect and confidence.

Not only is that a decision I came to regret, but it resulted in a period of my life that didn't feel meaningful or "fiction-like" and which I felt no desire to write about. Even though I got into some interesting situations as a result (trying to get myself beaten up, diving naked into the fountains at Hyde Park one night, etc.), it really does just feel like a bunch of random, meaningless stuff, and there also wasn't some great epiphany where I realised how stupid I was acting. I just gradually got over it, and about the only thing I learned was to try not to go out with crazy types in future, which I kind of knew already.

There've been other times I've ignored my instincts which also led to a lot of problems and no useful life lessons. So as with the essay on songwriting, I feel like I'm learning about instinct from what I myself wrote on the subject (instinctively?), and I've started trying to apply this to everything I do, where and when I go out, who I speak to, etc., which maybe explains why so much odd stuff seems to have been happening lately and this odd feeling of "everything turning in on itself" and "life imitating art imitating life."

Instinct was also a theme of the book on where science, religion and philosophy meet that I put on hold to write this one.

At one point I refer to it in relation to evolutionary theory and mention a fascinating native of the Australian Outback, called the mallee fowl or "incubator bird."

About the size of a small turkey, it gets its name from the towering structures it builds to incubate its eggs, which are too large and plentiful to manage by the standard method. It starts building the system the autumn prior to the laying season by digging a deep hole with its tiny feet which it then fills with leaves and vegetation scraped from the surrounding area. Come the rainy season the vegetation starts to rot and ferment, creating the basic heatsource for the system, and then in spring it starts piling on earth and sand until the structure is around 6 meters high.

It is now ready for the eggs which the female begins laying one every three to four days for the next six or seven months – making a total of around 36. Desert temperatures change hugely between day and night as well as through the seasons, and the eggs must be maintained at a constant 91F - a fluctuation of a single degree is enough to kill all of them.

So the mallee fowl rises each dawn, and using a beak that acts as both a thermometer and a barometer, it first gauges what the weather will be like that day and the temperature within the mound and then calculates if it needs to be lowered or raised. If it needs lowering, it starts drilling a series of cooling air vents, and if it needs to be raised, it lays out sand to warm under the sun, which it later spreads on top of the mound. It continues monitoring the situation throughout the day, laying out more sand or drilling more vents depending on what is required. When finally the eggs hatch, the chicks leave the same day, never to return. Kids, eh?

This is an extremely simplified description; the full process is far more complex, which from a scientific point of view raises some challenging questions. Not least why it didn't simply evolve to lay fewer or smaller eggs. There's also the issue of how it knows to build and operate such an incredibly complex system given they aren't around their parents long enough to observe the process. (Mallee fowl are also notoriously shy and will even run from others of their species.)

A biologist will of course say they know all this through instinct, but we know almost nothing about the mechanism behind it, where this knowledge is stored (the brain? its DNA? some form of collective consciousness?) or how it is passed on.

What I'm personally curious about is how all this works from the point of view of the mallee fowl. For example, when first digging the hole, how does it know when it's deep enough and time to start scraping in the vegetation? Or later, how high to pile the sand, how many vents to drill, how much sand to lay out, etc.?

And given it probably hasn't even seen an egg at this point, does it even know why it's doing all of this or the mound's ultimate purpose? And if not, why bother? There must be more enjoyable ways to spend its days than slaving from dusk to dawn for months on end.

My guess is that it doesn't know and is acting purely on a set of impulses. One day it just wakes up with an overwhelming urge to dig a hole. At some point the urge subsides and is replaced by a new one to scrape in bits of leaves and vegetation. The same happens when piling on the earth, and when the eggs are finally laid, it gets a new urge to put its beak in the air or into the mound, and depending on how that makes it feel, it then wants to drill some holes, lay out sand, etc.

And the reason it doesn't just lounge around in the sun all day is because if it did it would have this constant nagging feeling of work to be done and wouldn't be able to enjoy it.

And this is how Instinct gets us to do all of its hard work. Not by making every part of the process fun, but by making it impossible to feel good if you don't do it. So you end up just getting on with it.

It's only when the cute, fluffy chicks start hatching that "the wisdom becomes apparent" and the hard work feels worth it.

Which is also how I'm starting to feel about this book. I didn't really know why I began it; I just felt a strong urge. And while some of it's been hard and I've had some doubts along the way (see

'Ames, Aims and Amie'), now that I'm approaching the end, I'm starting to see "the wisdom" and I'm very glad I stuck with it.

Because it's become quite autobiographical, I've been thinking lately of how to join some gaps and tie up some loose ends. As I've written about both Holmewood and Downside, I thought I should write about the school I went to after, and I went to the cafe earlier to start on it. It was more out of duty than a genuine desire, and unsurprisingly, it wasn't really working and I ended up giving up on it.

Then Amie appeared (she didn't have to go back to Australia in the end). Without saying anything, she handed me an envelope and walked out. Inside was £100 in cash, which I realised was the proceeds of a bet we took a few days ago over some song that was playing in a bar. I considered giving it back to her, but she was the one who suggested it (originally for £50), and when I tried to dissuade her, she told me it was because I was afraid of losing and insisted we double it. Plus, it's Saturday and I fancy a night on the town.

But I still had to complete an essay, so I started writing about the bet, but didn't know where to take it. I then started thinking about all the strange stuff that has been going on, so I wrote about that, which led to the bit about instinct and the mallee fowl, but I got stuck on that too.

As I was trying to work out how to make it all work, it hit me that I was trying to tie the bet to the mallee fowl so I could go out courtesy of another Australian bird, and I realised I had my ending. Do you see what I mean about "weird shit?"

CHEYLESMORE

Sun 22 Oct

A recurring problem at Moravian was that everyone kept inviting their friends to stay, until we'd have half a dozen people crashed out each night and a permanent two-foot pile of washing-up that no one would claim any responsibility for. So at Cheylesmore we made a rule no one could stay without everyone else's permission, and we even managed to implement a cleaning rota.

    It was still pretty mad, though. Once Julie and I went to some Andy Warhol exhibition and dropped some acid to enhance the experience. It didn't really come on until we were heading back, though. As we were coming back into the block, Julie called over to one of the ex-Moravian guys, an older hippie known as "Acid John," to join us for a smoke. Inside our flat Jim was getting stoned with Gene October (I'd been kicked out of Chelsea by this point, but we continued to hang out), plus Mark and Rob, two dealer friends who'd just come back from their supplier and were each sitting with a pillowcase-sized bag of grass.

    After about ten minutes, there was still no sign of Acid John, so Julie suggested we give him another shout. We were standing on the balcony when apparently from nowhere two cops appeared. Pointing to our open front door, one of them asked if we lived there. With the acid kicking in, neither of us could think how to respond. Without replying, we both just stepped back inside and pulled the door shut.

    We told the others there were cops outside, and suddenly it was this farcical scene with everyone running around trying to decide whether to stay or leave and what to do with their dope. The funniest was Gene, who despite having just bought some tiny five quid deal (the smallest Mark would sell him), was panicking more than anyone and ended up tipping it into the bath before legging it out the front. Rob also left (with his bag stuffed under his jumper), while Mark decided to sit it out with us. A few minutes later Acid John knocked. He hadn't seen any cops, and we slowly began to relax and enjoy the rest of our trip.

Later we saw Nico at the Chelsea Town Hall (it seemed to have been a Factory-themed day). By the time we got back, Jim had learned the full story on what the cops were doing and how they seemed to appear from nowhere - they were in the process of busting our neighbours Tony and Kieron, having spotted some small pot plants growing in their window.

After packing them up for evidence, one asked Kieron if they had any other drugs in the flat. He assured them they hadn't, but using his cop's intuition, the other one went to their mantlepiece and picked up some boxing trophy under which was a quarter-ounce lump of hash.

"Okay, but that really is it," Kieron said and invited them to search the rest of the place if they wanted. Luckily, they believed him, as unbeknown to everyone, after leaving our flat and seeing their front door open, Rob had decided to pop his big bag of grass behind it to retrieve later once things had cooled down.

One can only imagine what would have happened had they found it.

"I swear, Officer, I've never seen that before."

"Oh, right. And I suppose someone just happened to be passing and decided to leave a huge bag of grass behind your door."

We lasted six months in the first flat at Cheylesmore and a further nine months in a two-floor place that became empty after that when the block went the same way as Moravian (only to sit vacant for another two years when the developers finally started selling the flats off at a huge profit).

BEACON

Mon 23 Oct 2006

If Holmewood was like a holiday camp compared to Downside, my last school Beacon would have resembled one even compared to Butlins. Classes ended at 3.30pm, there were no compulsory sports or meals, and as a sixth-former I could even wear what I liked.

It was also much more civilised than I was expecting. At Downside there was so much thieving that you couldn't even leave your books unattended. It was only when someone asked why I carried mine wherever I went that I began to realise just how fucked up it had been. ("But why would someone want to steal your schoolbooks?")

Best of all, it was mixed. There's nothing like a cute girl sitting a few desks away to brighten up a dull class. Not that any showed me much interest. Yet another drawback to boarding school is that you're packed off just around the time you're becoming interested in the opposite sex and would normally be developing some social skills. You'd try to make up for it in the holidays, but in the same way domestic cats are shunned by wild ones, people seemed to sense we were different just from how we moved and would instinctively stay away.

I found myself in awe of how socially relaxed the other guys were and their apparent experience. (I'd managed a couple of drunken fumblings, but had yet to go the whole way.) It was something I'd have to figure out if I didn't want to spend the rest of my life as one of those awkward bumbling ex-public school types.

As soon as I'd arrived, Richard, the drummer friend who'd recommended the school, introduced me to the only bassist he knew, a punk guy called Will. I should really say 'the only person who owned a bass' - a custom green thing, though he rarely played it. We got as far as playing a short assembly gig when it became clear Will had taken his rock star ambitions as far as he wanted and gave up practising altogether.

We advertised for a replacement, but there was just no one available - or at least no one into the same kind of music. Then Richard and I had a falling out. Drummers were in even shorter supply than bassists. I continued to practise and write, but if I was in any doubt about moving to London, I was now almost counting the minutes.

I'd chosen sociology for one of my A levels, mainly because I'd heard it was easy and the classes were full of girls, but I ended up really getting into it thanks to a great teacher called Mr Barratt who would illustrate the various theories with little comic routines and anecdotes from his bachelor days. We'd often debate the subject during break times, which is how I became friends with Adam.

As well as being the funniest guy in school, he was also the best looking and, consequently, had just about every hot girl after him, if he hadn't been with them already. (He also had a car.) I once asked how you made the leap from talking to kissing, and he said you just felt it. Maybe girls just didn't like me.

I'd finally got to try dope at least when someone passed me a joint at some local rock festival. You had to be very discrete on the subject back then. To many people cannabis was no different to heroin. Eventually, I breached the subject with Adam by asking if he fancied trying some.

"Sure," he said, "anything to relieve the boredom" - which

surprised me coming from the most popular guy in the school.

We managed to find a dealer and were soon getting stoned every weekend, mainly via "hot knives" using a Calor Gas stove Adam kept in the back of his Mini.

There's an interview with Gerry Garcia of the Grateful Dead where he points to a joint he's holding and says something like, "Basically the more people smoke of this, the better the world will be," and that was how we saw it. We made it our mission to get everyone in our sociology class to try it (we persuaded all but one).

When the mushroom season came, we also got into that in a big way. We had some hilarious and magical trips driving down tunnel-like country lanes with Syd Barrett-era Pink Floyd bouncing between the back speakers."Travelling by telephone, yippee - you can't see me, but I...can...you." It was like our own personal '60s. We even stood in a school election as The Transcendental Reactionary Party on a ticket of pure hedonism, coming in third, just behind the Liberals.

I no longer see drugs in such a benign light. I still think they can offer valuable insights if taken on occasion or for a short period. But that's hard to stick to in reality, and the longer one takes them, the more their negative aspects become apparent - which are usually the reverse of whatever it was you liked about them. If they give you energy, you end up more lethargic. If they make you sociable, you feel more withdrawn. If they numb some pain (mental or physical), you feel it more acutely. Etc.

So rather than a kind of something-for-nothing deal, as I and people like Gerry Garcia thought, it's more akin to a kind of happiness overdraft facility - it must all be paid back at some point, plus a little on top (the bank always charges interest). This applies to all drugs, even something as mild as a cup of coffee. It's just more obvious with the stronger stuff.

The negative effects can take a few days to manifest, or you just feel a bit under par in the days or weeks after taking them,* obscuring their damage.

(*Terms and conditions may vary.*)

Some drugs may be taken for years before their negative effects become apparent, lulling the user into a false sense of security. Tobacco and "soft" drugs can be particularly insidious in this respect. By the time the problems are obvious, they may have become integrated into one's lifestyle, making them even harder to give up.

The longer one takes a drug, the more one's natural endorphins and "happy" chemicals start to diminish, worsening both the highs and the lows. To counter this, a user may increase their intake and/or switch to another, possibly harder, drug. This is like taking out a high-interest loan to pay off a smaller debt, driving one even deeper "into the red." Quitting then becomes harder still, and there may be a long period of listlessness to endure before one's happy chemicals are replenished. Instead of accepting this as the inevitable consequence of sustained use, some take it as evidence of how drab life is without their drug of choice and return to it with renewed enthusiasm. It's often not until their health is affected that they accept the truth, by which time it may be too late.

I found it much harder to enjoy drugs after seeing them in these terms, but I was naïve to that back then and still having a fantastic time blowing my overdraft.

Given how blasé we'd become, it was inevitable word would eventually get back to the teachers. I'd given myself the afternoon off when a panicked-sounding Adam rang to say the Headmaster had asked to see him and he'd heard it was connected to our habits. As we'd always taken it together, he said he was bound to want to see me too, and unless I wanted to also be done for cutting school, I should get down there asap.

When I got to the Headmaster's office, Adam was still waiting to be called in. Eventually, he came out and signalled for me to come in.

"It's interesting to find you here," he said, "as I didn't actually ask to see you." Doh!

He knew I was involved, though, and I have to say was extremely reasonable about the whole thing, saying what we did outside school was none of his business, but if we came in high or involved a younger pupil, it would be and he'd have no choice but to expel us. (We found out later that a fifth-form girl Adam brought to one of our sessions had told her parents.)

We made it to the end of the year without getting into trouble, and I left with three okay passes (better than I deserved given I'd spent the week of my exams building a bubble machine out of a hair dryer and some Meccano).

I'd still yet to go all the way with a girl. However, I'd picked up a tip from my neighbour that would eventually lead to it. He mentioned some guy at his college who he said pulled more girls than anyone else by simply asking every single one that he liked the look of for a date. He'd go up to them in shops, buses, literally everywhere. Most turned him down, but every now and again one would say "yes," and that was enough to keep him inundated. So along with my ridiculous vow to sleep rough in London before returning home to ask for help, I made another that I'd speak to any girl I really liked. The "throw enough mud" approach became my modus operandi for a few years, until I began refining my technique and thinking of more sophisticated methods.

POLL TAX RIOTS

Tues 24 Oct 2006

The chance of finding any more upmarket squats after Cheylesmore seemed very remote, but we weren't giving up just yet. Julie and I nearly struck gold when we were offered a whole floor of Keith Richards' old mansion on Cheyne Walk, but there was no running water or electricity, so we decided to keep looking. (To deter squatters it was becoming increasingly common for landlords to rip out wiring and rip out plumbing. Even the council had started doing this.)

Then Kieron opened a semi-derelict privately owned house off the King's Road and said we could have the basement. It was cold water only and pretty icey, but we made it nice.

As much as I liked Julie, I wasn't in love and never meant things to get so serious. I tried ending it a few times, but neither of us had anywhere to move to, and it's not easy sharing a room/bed with someone you've just broken up with. After a couple of hours of sobbing, I'd always end up agreeing to give it yet one more try. Then my sister offered me a cheap room in a place she'd bought in Shepherd's Bush, and seeing my escape route, I took it.

I was there for about a year when I was put in touch with an Australian girl called Courtney whose landlord had just fled the country to escape some debts, leaving the house she'd been living in caught in an ownership dispute between the mortgage company and his bank. With no one to pay rent to, she'd decided to claim squatting status and was looking for people with experience to move in.

Though I didn't have to move, a rent-free pad in Notting Hill was too much to resist, and of all the squats I'd lived in, it proved to be the most fun. By the time it was filled, there was me, Paul, the bassist I was now playing with, a radio DJ called Dave and, including Courtney, no less than nine girls! If that wasn't enough, one of them had obsessive compulsive disorder forcing her to clean all the communal areas before breakfast! I'd also recently been passed on a part-time job delivering air tickets in the West End, so I actually had some spare cash for the first time.

This was all happening at the tail end of the 1980s and about halfway through the Conservatives' third term under Margaret Thatcher. Depending who you ask, you'll get a very different account of life in Britain back then. To higher professionals, businessmen, investors, etc., it was a golden time with "Maggie" a saviour figure who'd rescued the country from the clutches of the unions, slashed the upper rates of tax and removed business red tape. Her privatisation programme had led to various state-owned industries being sold off well below market value, allowing for regular easy killings on the stock exchange. The sale of over 1.5 million council homes had even won her support among many Labour voters which, combined with a relaxation of rental controls, helped fuel a massive property boom.

But while properties tripled in value in a few short years and City workers toasted record bonuses, for those at the bottom of the scale, life had pretty much been one long downward slide since the Tories came to office.

The tax cuts had to be funded somehow, and it was mostly through a drastic reduction in public spending, meaning reduced grants and pensions, pay freezes or below inflation rises for nurses, teachers, firemen, etc., and libraries, museums, galleries, etc., having to close or introduce charges. This was on top of the soaring rents and more expensive/ever-deteriorating public services caused by the sell-offs - all of which impacted hardest on the poor.

The Tories had also presided over a huge surge in unemployment, from around 1.5 million when taking office to almost 4 million. The figure would have been even higher if not for over 30 changes to how it was calculated - all resulting in a reduction. The most cynical of these was to change the definition of "unemployed" from "out of work" to "out of work *and receiving benefit.*" This instantly removed tens of thousands from the books who were ineligible for whatever reasons (e.g., having a partner in work or savings over £1,200), while increasing their incentive to make the process as difficult as possible (a single error in the 40-page signing-on form could see your claim denied), or to throw them onto some Mickey Mouse training scheme.

The bulk of the job losses were in manufacturing, devastating once-proud communities and turning swathes of the country into heroin-ravaged wastelands.

In response to the problem, the then-Employment Secretary Norman Tebbit famously said that in his father's day, people had "got on their bikes" and looked for work. They were just lazy, in other words. The remark was felt like a slap in the face by the millions who'd lost their livelihoods through no fault of their own, and it was as ignorant as it was heartless. Even in the capital, there was little apart from menial stuff that paid a pittance which people were still fighting for. I'd got lucky with my delivery job, but before that I'd advertised myself as a cleaner at £2.50 p.h. and never found more than four hours a week. A girl I was seeing applied for a £1 p.h. waitressing job (with no breaks), and there were so many applicants, she was kept waiting an hour for her interview.

Nevertheless, "the jobs are out there" would become the official government mantra, and it was depressing how many bought into it. Through my sister I'd occasionally get invited to dinner parties where there'd be a few professional types, lawyers, doctors, journos, etc., and was witness to more than one post-dinner diatribe about work-shy layabouts "sponging off my taxes" and how there was plenty of work if people just got off their arses to look.

The resentment was being fuelled by the right wing, mostly Murdoch-owned, press* - a constant drip-feed of bile-filled headlines and editorials attacking benefit cheats (aka "dole-scrounging scum"), single mothers and any example they could find of the "something-for-nothing culture."

(*Murdoch had significantly expanded his media empire due to a personal intervention from Mrs Thatcher regarding monopoly laws - leading to suspicions some kind of deal had been struck in return for his unwavering support.)

The spending cuts had initially been justified as reducing waste and inefficiency, but as vital transport links began to disappear, schools, hospitals and even mental institutions began to close ("Care in the Community" as they dared call it). There was a growing feeling that the aim from the start was a systematic dismantling of the welfare state via the back door. Personal freedoms were also vanishing. Clause 28 made it an offence to 'promote' homosexuality (whatever that meant), while a public order act was being drafted forbidding gatherings of more than ten people without permission, effectively outlawing strikes and even private parties. There'd also been a big increase in the use of D-notices that barred the press from reporting on certain strikes and protests (usually those with rumours of police heavy-handedness).

All this led to an incredibly polarised and poisonous atmosphere. Since arriving in London, I'd save money by picking up discarded newspapers on bus seats, tops of bins, etc., until I'd notice perhaps a quarter of them torn into shreds. I almost never saw this before or after this time and can only explain it as people thinking; *I paid for my copy, I'm damned if someone else will have it for free* and a symptom of how mean-spirited people had become.

I don't know if there's some Machiavellian theory pointing out you can only lose a person's vote once, so as long as you only shit on one sector, you can hold power almost indefinitely. Anyway, that's how it seemed to have worked. Though loathed by millions, Thatcher had maintained enough loyal support to win three consecutive elections and with a big enough majority to pass every piece of legislation she'd introduced.

Where she miscalculated was the Community Charge, aka Poll Tax. Unlike the 'Rates', a household tax covering things like street lighting and rubbish collection which it was designed to replace, the Poll Tax was basically a flat charge that took no account of a person's income or size of their property. Great news for wealthy landowners, not so brilliant for families in small accommodation or OAPs living alone, some of whom faced a 300% increase for the same not-great-in-the-first-place services and big fines or even jail if they couldn't pay.

For the first time Thatcher was enacting a bill that would impact on many of her own supporters, and it was amazing how fast the mood changed once Middle England got a taste of what the rest of the country had been forced to swallow the previous decade. Sensing the shift, even the right-wing press joined calls for the tax to be abolished, while dinner parties across the land reverberated with a new angle on the situation and that while she had definitely done some great things for the country, perhaps the time had come for someone else to take the reins.

It was against this backdrop the Anti-Poll Tax Rally was born. Scheduled the day the first bills were due to arrive (April 1st no less), four separate marches were due to converge in one mass demonstration in Trafalgar Square.

I decided to head directly to the demo and arrived at Tottenham Court Road tube around 4pm. As I was coming out the entrance,

I happened to see our bassist Paul and his girlfriend who were on their way back. I asked what the atmosphere was like. "Great," he said, "really chilled." That sounds funny in retrospect, but at that point it was true. Though packed with demonstrators carrying "Axe the Tax" placards and chanting the now familiar "Maggie! Maggie! Maggie! Out! Out! Out!," people were smiling, and it was very relaxed.

I'd been there about 20 minutes when I noticed some people pointing to a street to the left side of the square where a line of cops plus a couple on horseback were pushing back at a group of protesters. Some bits of placards and a couple of empty plastic bottles were flying through the air, but whatever the problem, it didn't look that serious.

Then suddenly, police on our side started shouting through megaphones that we all had to leave. Apart from the fact I'd only just got there, I knew they had no right to break up a legal protest just because they felt like it and, along with hundreds of others, decided to stay put. The police then started pushing people physically, which just made everyone more determined to remain. Some of the cops began linking arms with their shields up, and before I knew what was happening, about 30 of us were being shoved against a wall. We were all crushed together, and it was obvious we couldn't move, but they kept pushing and shouting for us to get further back. We didn't have a choice but to push back, and eventually someone broke their line and we all poured through.

Scuffles were breaking out all around as police started grabbing whoever they could, while fending off others who tried to pull them away. To escape the trouble, a few people had climbed onto ledges and walls along Charing Cross Road, and I decided to join them.

As we watched the unfolding chaos, someone wandered up carrying a brick they'd found and then lobbed it at a high window of a bank opposite where I was sitting. It was obviously made of unbreakable glass as it just bounced off without so much as chipping it. Someone shouted for him to give it another go, but it bounced off again, followed by a disappointed "aah" from those watching. He kept trying, with each attempt followed by a louder "aah" from the crowd - no doubt all of us wondering the same thing - just how unbreakable is "unbreakable glass?" Finally it shattered to a loud cheer from the crowd, while the guy walked off with a big smile.

At some point I rejoined what was now a full-scale riot with other windows being broken and cars overturned (I saw one on fire). Mounted police had begun launching regular charges up and down Charing Cross Road, batonning anyone within reach. I took a hit from one, but luckily another cop's shield got in the way, absorbing most of the force.

To escape one of the charges, I ran down a side street past a couple of antique stamp and book shops which had also been ransacked - leaving collections strewn everywhere - and then into a Renault showroom which had all its windows smashed in and every car battered. Another guy ran in laughing his head off, "Can you fucking believe this?" he said.

I couldn't, but I no longer thought it funny as the vandalism had become completely indiscriminate. I imagined how the shop owners would feel when they came to find all those rare stamps and books ruined. I was also thinking how it would get reported and how easily the press could portray the demonstrators as nothing but mindless hooligans.

But a less high-minded and seemingly contradictory thought had occurred. I was only a couple of hundred yards from Denmark Street, where most of London's music shops were situated. If this was happening here, what might it be like there?

I wasn't looking to take advantage, merely curious (and when did curiosity get anyone into trouble?). Despite my squatting history and the "Buskers Will Be Prosecuted" sign, I was actually very moral when it came to personal theft. The only thing I'd ever taken from a shop was a Mars bar, and that was only because Nick (my first flatmate) shoved it into my hand as we were leaving because he knew my feelings and wanted to force me to lose my "shoplifting virginity."

The scene that greeted me was crazier than I could have imagined. Almost every instrument shop had been looted, and people were running around with guitars and saxophones under their arms, some holding two or three. There were hundreds of cops, but for some reason they seemed more interested in pushing back other protesters rather than tackling the looters.

As I approached one shop, a guy was holding up the shutter, allowing people to literally take what they wanted. I then spotted a couple of microphones on the ground still in their packaging. I'd recently bought a tape machine and was on the look-out for mics. So I started telling myself it wasn't really shoplifting if something was outside a shop. And if I left them, they'd probably end up getting stepped on and would be no use to anyone. Of course, I could have thrown them back inside, but I chose to ignore that thought and slipped them into my pocket.

As people continued helping themselves to various rare and beautiful guitars, I saw a cherry red Gibson 335 with F holes. I'd wanted a 335 for years, but at around £1,500 there was no way I could afford one. Having moved my moral goalposts, I now tried to justify outright theft. It was a big store, I told myself, not like one of the stamp or book shops. No one would be personally hurt, and they were bound to be fully insured.

As I stood there trying to convince myself, some scuzzy-looking character, who didn't even look like a guitarist, leaned in and grabbed it. What had my moral agonising achieved here? He'd probably sell it that night for the price of a heroin wrap. That settled it. The guy who'd been holding the shutter had got nervous and run off, so I pulled it back up myself and took the nicest guitar within reach - a signature semi-acoustic with a £750 tag.

As soon as it was in my hands, the adrenaline kicked in as it hit me I was in possession of a stolen guitar and two mics in a riot zone swarming with police. I put my coat over the guitar and made it home via a circuitous route and put on the news, which of course was full of the story.

As I'd feared, there was cross-party condemnation of the riots (the looting had apparently spread as far as Bond Street, including various gold and jewellery shops) with no mention it had been a peaceful protest until the cops started attacking everyone, and it was the same with next day's papers, even the left-leaning ones.

Although a very good guitar, it was intended for jazz, and I just couldn't get along with it. I'd have put it up for sale, but I knew the cops were doing all they could to recover the looted goods, so I started checking the "Instruments Wanted" ads. A couple of weeks later I saw one looking for the exact model to buy or trade for a Yamaha 335 - not as nice as the Gibson I originally wanted, but a decent copy.

I doubted the cops would place such a specific ad, but to be safe, I called from a phone box and arranged to meet at his. We tried each other's guitar, then agreed on a straight swap.

Just when I thought I was home free, he asked for a receipt so he could get it insured. I wrote one out using a false name and left with the Yamaha and a very bad conscience, knowing there was a strong chance it would come up as stolen. It was unlikely they'd try to prosecute him, but legally it would have to be returned to the shop, so I'd have effectively swindled him out of his guitar.

I felt so bad, I didn't even take it out of the case. The next morning I went back to the phone box and spun him a story about how I'd bought the guitar just after the riots and there was a tiny possibility that's where it came from, so insuring it might not be wise. I offered to swap guitars back or send him £100 as compensation.

"That's very kind of you to let me know," he said, "I think I'll take the cash." Should have said £50.

I got the money and went to the post office where a young blonde was serving.

"Hi. Erm, I was wondering if there's some way I can post £100 in cash securely without having to put my name and address on the envelope?"

"We can do that. But why wouldn't you want to give your details?"

I was expecting this.

"What it is, I've got this friend who's in a bad situation financially. I'd like to help him, but he's very proud, so I thought if I sent some cash anonymously, he'd have no choice but to accept it."

She looked at me stunned. "Oh...my...God!!! I didn't think men like you still existed!" I think if I'd asked, she'd probably have married me on the spot.

At least I didn't take advantage.

A few months later, Thatcher was kicked out by her own party and then replaced by John Major, who somehow managed to win them another term. A lot of people think the riots were her downfall. I think the Poll Tax was, but if anything, the actual riots probably bought her some time. The fact I played a part in that is not something I'm proud of.

That said, the gear proved very useful. I used one of the mics to record 'Girl at the Bus Stop' and the guitar for the *This Is My Drug Hell* album.

MY DRUG HELL - THE EARLY YEARS

Wed 25 Oct 2006

I've been meaning to tell the full story of My Drug Hell, so I should probably get on with it. After getting kicked out of Chelsea, I decided to put a band together based around my own songs and started going through the music paper ads. One of the first people I tried was a guitarist from Essex called Karl. He liked my stuff, and despite some reservations, I agreed to give it a go.

For the most part, Karl was a really easy-going guy who liked nothing more than practising in front of the TV with a six pack of lager and the heating turned up to full, but he also had a darker side which I'd get occasional intimations of. Once he told me sheepishly he'd gone "a bit mad" the night before and explained a group of guys had been eyeing up his girlfriend in a pub on Lavender Hill. He waited for them outside with an iron bar he'd found somewhere and ended up swinging it around his head going, "So come on, lads - who wants it first?"

I've noticed musicians play like their personalities, and it was very true in his case. Most of the time he'd play these laid-back, bordering-on-insipid blues runs, but then out of nowhere would launch into some blistering, demonically inspired solo that left me floored. I'd ask him to play it exactly as he'd done it, but he'd have been so in the moment he wouldn't even know which part of the neck he'd played it on and would go back to the Test Card noodlings. It was pretty frustrating, but we'd occasionally capture a good one on tape and gradually built up a set.

In the meantime, I'd found a great bassist from New Zealand

called Chris. Unfortunately, he decided to return home without bothering to tell us. Then Karl met another Kiwi bass player called Paul on the building site where he worked and invited him to audition. He kept saying stuff like, "We can't afford to let this one go," as if he'd already decided to take him. Knowing how impulsive he could be, I got him to agree not to give him a definite "yes" or "no" until we'd discussed it privately.

We went through a couple of songs with him, and it was obvious he hadn't been playing very long. He also had a very driving style I wasn't wild about. Karl went to make some tea, and when he got back, he turned to Paul.

"Well, as far as I'm concerned, mate - you're in the band!"

They both turned to me.

"...Er...yeah...I suppose."

Later, I told Karl my concerns, and he said we should give it a couple more rehearsals and let him go if I was still unhappy. The next was a little better, and he continued to improve, so we stuck with it.

As well as checking adverts, I'd been going up to musician-looking types at gigs, clubs, etc. If they didn't play or were already in a band, I'd ask if they knew anyone who might suit us, which was how we found our drummer, Chris Calvert.

Our first gig was as The Atomic Vicars supporting Chelsea at the Marquee. We went down pretty well, though Karl was still changing or forgetting his parts. We'd go into a chorus, and he'd still be soloing away oblivious.

We played another 20 or so gigs, but the problems weren't going away. Apparently, he had his own grievances as the day we planned to tell him he was out, he rang to say he was leaving. Phew.

We had some gigs booked that I was reluctant to cancel, so we did them as a three-piece with me filling in for Karl as best I could. I gradually adapted my style until people stopped saying we could use a fourth member, and we decided to continue as we were.

I'd always assumed that if a band was good and played regularly, you'd gradually build a following. That may have been true in the '60s and '70s, but there were now many more bands around and, thanks to changes in the music licensing laws, only about a dozen venues worth playing. Unless you already had a name, they'd usually offer you some dead 9pm on a Tuesday slot with the promise of a better one if you brought enough people. Even your biggest fans don't want to come to every gig, and because you'd been given such a shitty slot, it was almost impossible to gain any new ones. So you'd actually end up playing to fewer people the more often you played. The only way to break the cycle was to get a deal or a journalist on your side. I was constantly calling people and sending out demos, but after three years and a hundred gigs, not one label had even come to see us and the only press we'd had was a small live review in Melody Maker.

Then one day an angel appeared in the form of a friend/fan called George Mansell. Out of the blue he handed us a cheque for £1,000. He didn't even want it back. He just said he believed in us and wanted to help.

We agreed to spend it on releasing our own 7". A singing teacher Paul knew asked if she could produce us, and I let myself be talked into booking two days in a 24-track studio in East London. It was a disaster from start to finish. Having tried to get us all to change our parts, we finally got two songs down and were about to lay down a mix when Chris made some comment about how his headphones had been distorting, which the owner took as a personal attack. He suddenly pulled all the faders down and announced the session was over. It took a couple of months before he gave me the tapes back, and because he'd used some outdated noise reduction system, there was nowhere we could get them mixed.

We had just enough money left for a day and half in a cheap demo studio where we finished two tracks and then had 500 copies pressed. It was too little too late for Chris, though, who told us he was leaving to join some glam metal act.

We placed some ads and eventually found a replacement, Tim (aka Joe) Bultitude. He wasn't as technical a player as Chris, but he had a lazy, behind-the-beat style I liked, and the music seemed to take on a much more emotional edge after he joined.

I'd been mailing out the 7"s to almost no response when I received a letter from Kramer, head of the cult US label Shimmydisc, who'd been passed on a copy. He described one of the songs as "one of the most heartfelt ballads I've ever heard" and asked if we'd record an album for the label at his studio in New York.

I immediately called him and said we'd love to do it. However, I'd just discovered a vintage studio in London called Toe Rag that I was very keen to use. We agreed that if I covered studio costs, he'd release it. (It so happened my grandmother had died two weeks before and I was due to receive £1,500 from her will - enough for five rehearsals and a week of studio time.) I also told him we'd changed our name to My Drug Hell.

I rang the others and suggested a night on the town to celebrate. Joe made an excuse, and a couple of days later called to say he was leaving as he didn't feel the music was right for him.

By this point I'd put down a deposit for Toe Rag, so we placed a couple of ads, yielding just four responses, none of which were remotely suitable. About ten days before the booking I rang Joe to see if he'd reconsider.

"Oh, what the hell? I don't see why not!"

We'd allocated 2½ days to record the basic tracks, 2½ for all vocals and overdubs and 2 days to mix. Kramer wanted 16 songs, so we'd have to work hard.

The first day went well. Liam (the engineer) got a good sound, and we recorded about six takes. About halfway through the next day we started on a song called 'You Were Right, I Was Wrong,' which for some reason wasn't coming together. Joe and Paul said I was to blame and that they should record a take of just them for me to then overdub my part. I thought it was the wrong approach, but it was two votes to one. Once they'd got a take, they went to lunch, leaving me to add my guitar.

Not only did the groove feel wrong, but there was a timing mistake I couldn't find a way around. When they returned, I explained the problem. Joe suddenly exploded that the version was fine and I just wasn't up to the job, "...and it's a crap song, anyway." I bit my tongue and suggested we give it two more tries with us all playing together, and we ended up keeping the first. It's still my favourite track, and as angry as I felt, I don't think it would have come out as well if not for the argument. It made us all determined not to be the one to fuck up and gave it an atmosphere of genuine tension and mutual resentment that perfectly suited the subject matter. There's a particularly effective snare shot Joe put in near the end that always makes me think of a plate thrown against a wall.

Things calmed down after that, and by the end of the week, we had all the tracks done, and I sent a copy to Kramer.

After a few weeks without a response, I called him up, and he said he hadn't received it. It sounded strange, but I sent another copy. A few more weeks and many unreturned messages later, I finally got through and had my fears confirmed. "I'm real sorry, man, but it wasn't what I was expecting. I can't release it." (As compensation, he did end up releasing a 7" single, but with no promotion, and it sank without a trace.)

I'd been sending out tapes of the best five tracks and getting some good reactions, but no firm offers. Then one day I popped into the Music and Video Exchange in Notting Hill where someone was trading in a reel to reel. I whispered that I might be able to offer him a better price, but he said he'd already agreed one. He introduced himself as Sean, and we got chatting. He said he'd recently set up a studio in Ealing and invited me to check it out.

A few days later I went round. He mentioned he was also setting up a label and asked if I had anything I could play him. I made sure I always had a tape on me, and he put it on. Almost immediately he started raving about the sound, and by the third song had offered us a record deal. He then asked if I had any other tracks I could play him. I said there were a couple of solo recordings on the other side, the first of which was 'Girl at the Bus Stop.' Literally within a minute he was going, "This is it! This is the fucking single!" He played it again and then called in a couple of his staff saying, "You have got to hear this!"

It was one of those biopic moments I'd spent my life dreaming of. Three days later he had a contract drawn up and we signed to Diversity Recordings.

By now it was clear that not all the tracks were fully up to scratch or they needed remixing or fixes. Sean suggested Diversity release a 7" of 'Girl at the Bus Stop' while I worked on what needed doing.

About a week after they sent out the white label promos, Radio 1's Evening Session picked it up and then started playing it every night. It also started getting daytime plays on XFM and GLR, and it was Single of the Week on a couple of shows. It was very exciting; however no one had anticipated such a fast response. The official singles weren't pressed up yet. We hadn't even designed the artwork - and we also needed a video.

I'd been experimenting with a Super 8 camera and was friends with a photographer called Claudia who also had one as well as access to lights and an editing suite belonging to her father, Vic. I told Sean we could make the video ourselves for £350, which he agreed to. We decided to shoot a basic band performance against a backdrop at Vic's, followed by some outdoor shots of us around

London as well as buses, etc., to cut in.

On the day of the band shoot, Claudia started setting up the film equipment while Paul and I set up the band gear. Joe had asked if he could get there when we were done, so I said to be there for 2pm. As soon as Claudia began checking the lights, she found around half weren't working. She called in Vic who said they'd all worked a week before. Super 8 needs a lot of light, and we barely had enough to get a reading on the meter.

We then discovered our one sound camera wasn't accepting cartridges for some reason. I'd already been told it was almost impossible to lip sync with Super 8. Now it would be even harder.

By 3pm, Joe still hadn't arrived. I'd called him at home several times to find out when he'd left, but no one picked up. Finally around 4pm, Joe himself answered.

"You're still at home? What's going on?"

"I've decided I'm leaving the band."

"For fuck's sake! You could at least have told us yesterday."

He then got abusive, and I said goodbye.

Claudia suggested we start packing up, but we had to have some kind of video, so I began ringing anyone I could think of who could act as a stand-in. No one was available, except Ian (the ex-Cool Rays singer I talked about in 'How The Music Industry Destroyed Rock 'n' Roll') who said he could film the outdoor stuff we'd planned for that weekend.

He had a similar build and hair colour to me, so I then came up with a work-around whereby we'd film the band performance with just myself and Paul plus a bit of the drum kit visible. Then we'd get some brief cutaways of me behind the drums with shades and my hair back to look as different as possible. If we mixed that with some outdoor stuff plus Ian, it might just be possible to make it look like a full band. The others were up for it, and I went to mime my vocals, looking as happy-go-lucky as I could manage, having just learned we were drummer-less again at such a crucial time.

After the outdoor shoot, we sent the films to the labs and a few weeks later got them back. A lot of the footage was under-exposed or blurry, but we reckoned we had enough usable stuff for a 3 ½-minute video and booked a day at Vic's with his editor.

She spent a couple of hours logging the time codes of every shot and then wound to the one we wanted to start with of a foot hitting the bass drum – only to find a completely different one in its place. She began looking for other shots, but it was the same thing, as if the time codes were just randomly moving around and making it impossible to locate anything.

As she tried to figure out the problem, various error codes started flashing on the playback VTR, "Error 2," "Error 5," "Error 3," etc. - each signifying a different problem. Then it began happening on the record VTR, which was particularly strange as the two units weren't directly connected. Then both monitor screens started flicking on and off.

She called in Vic, who was completely baffled at how so many different pieces of equipment could start malfunctioning simultaneously. He rang his engineer, but he said he couldn't come in until the following week. I'd told Sean we'd have the video by that weekend, so I called a secretary at the label who somehow found an editor willing to finish it for £80 (all that remained from the budget).

A few minutes later, the editor came in to say she'd managed to sync up the first shot to the music. Although we knew we'd be finishing the video elsewhere, we were curious to see how it would look. She pressed "play" and we saw a brief image of a kick drum, followed by a strange watery sound as the machine chewed up the tape (not the master, luckily).

The second editor worked out great, and I got the video to Sean on time and within the budget. No one noticed the various continuity issues, and it ended up winning a Best Video vote on

MTV's Alternative Nation.

Unfortunately, by the time it was available to buy, most of the airplay had died down. It still managed three months in the indie charts, but it was hard not to wonder how it would have fared had the timing been better.

A couple of months later Joe returned and Diversity released a 7" of 'You Were Right, I Was Wrong,' which made Number 5 in Melody Maker's indie chart. Again, it would probably have done better if not for a flood at the pressing plant ensuring it wouldn't be in the shops until a couple of months after the initial push.

This would have been a good time to release the album. The problem I had was that word about Toe Rag's unique sound had got out and it now had a waiting list of around three months. If I didn't manage to complete what needed doing, it would be another three months before I could get back in. I didn't even have a way to check the tapes to see what needed doing, so I ended up buying an old ¼" tape machine so I could at least check the various mixes.

I started to go through them and began noticing an occasional volume drop-out. When I rechecked it, I'd sometimes find another one. By the time I realised it was the machine itself that was inflicting them, around half the mixes were ruined.

We'd also been having problems with the artwork. A journalist had asked to borrow the front cover transparency for some feature. Despite promising to be especially careful, he actually managed to lose it. Using an alternative shot, we went to a design studio where the computer started behaving very strangely and then shut down completely. It was just like at Vic's with the owner looking completely mystified and saying it all worked perfectly before we got there. We then went to another studio where more or less the same thing happened.

At some point I'd joked in an interview about the "Curse of My Drug Hell," but as disasters and equipment breakdowns seemed to follow our every move (seven broken strings during one gig), others began referring to it.

Finally, we were one track away from the album being complete. We all felt the version we had of 'Jinx's Hole' wasn't as good as we were playing it live. We recorded a new version in a semi-vintage place in Chiswick and another in Diversity's own studios, but neither were an improvement, so I ended up trying to spruce up the original with a couple of overdubs and a new vocal.

It was all done except for a couple of lines that needed fixing when Liam said he had to pop out for a bit and put his new assistant in charge. I told him we should wait until Liam got back, but he insisted he could manage them. I put the headphones on ready to sing the first one, but couldn't hear the line before - he'd dropped in too early and erased it.

He then managed to erase another line which included a spontaneous shout I'd really liked. By the time we'd fixed all his fuck-ups, plus the bits I'd wanted to do originally, there wasn't enough time to finish the mix. It was a couple of months before I got back in, but finally both the album and artwork were ready and a release date was set.

Two weeks before the date, Diversity Recordings ceased trading. And two days after that, Joe quit again.

Mercifully, Diversity had by now licensed the album to labels in both the US and Australia, and it was starting to pick up some very good reviews. It ended up having a long run in the US college charts and made their national Specialty Show Top 10.

'Bus Stop' was also getting a lot of college play and became Number 1 Most Requested on all three commercial stations that put it on their playlist – including a 10-week run on WHTG, prompting its owner to fax 50 other stations saying he'd never had such a response to an unknown band (five times as many requests as for anyone else) and urging them to play it.

We were then told Miller beer wanted to use it for a TV

commercial. I'd specifically instructed our manager not to give it to ads, but we were still without a deal in the UK, and despite the US label taking 95% of the money, it allowed us to release the single '2am.' When Miller ran the ad in the UK, we re-released 'Bus Stop' which Mark Goodier made his Single of the Weekend on Radio 1. They still didn't add it to their playlist, though, and again it seemed to just miss becoming a bona fide hit.

In the meantime, Joe had rejoined and quit a couple more times, the last occasion three days before a gig. Luckily, we'd just found Raife who got us through it.

We then released a 7" of 'Maybe We Could Fly' (500 copies pressed at the wrong speed) along with a video that was an even bigger nightmare to edit than 'Bus Stop' involving three editors and several complete losses of data. I liked the result, though, and it got a year's worth of rotation on VH1.

Having to deal with Joe's constant coming and going meant other issues had been neglected, but we'd been having almost as many problems with Paul, culminating in the bust-up I mentioned in the 'Kelly' essay.

We found a French bassist called Seb plus a new manager, Des, but the "Curse" continued to plague us. After sending out 50 demo CDs to all his industry contacts, Des received a call from the producer of TFI Friday suggesting he check them. Thanks to yet another pressing plant cock-up, they'd somehow pressed up ten tracks of monks chanting!

For some reason the second line-up never quite worked - we could rock, but we couldn't roll, to borrow a Keith Richards line. We made half a dozen attempts to record a follow-up album when Raife decided to cut his losses and quit.

While looking to replace Paul, I'd returned to my old method of going up to people on the street, etc., and got talking to a German guy on Portobello Road, another Seb. He seemed cool, but he was a drummer, not a bassist. The day after Raife left, I saw him again and asked if he wanted to try out. He had the slightly lazy style I liked, and he was into the music.

Meanwhile, French Seb was dealing with a girlfriend problem in Paris that meant we'd barely seen him in months, so reluctantly we had to let him go. I checked the music paper ads, and the first guy I rang, an Australian called Dave, turned out to be both a very good player and a really nice guy.

I'd never had a line-up come together so easily. It's taken some time to completely gel, but we seem to be there now and are close to finally finishing our follow-up. Perhaps the Curse has been lifted.

DIGGING FOR SQUIRRELS
or
HOW I BECAME A SMART-ARSE

Thurs 26 Oct 2006

My earliest memory is being pushed in my pram down Church Road, Crowborough by my grandmother (the same one who left the money that paid for *This Is My Drug Hell*). Every now and again she'd let go of the handle allowing me to freewheel for a couple of seconds before catching it - while I'd be giggling and gurgling and willing her to do it again.

I once checked this story with my grandmother, thinking I may have imagined it. She confirmed she used to do this, though her abiding memory was what would happen when we reached the crossroads a little further down. In front was a relatively picturesque spot called Chapel Green, but whenever she tried to take me across, I'd grab the left side of my pram and start making these angry, grunting noises, signalling I wanted to be taken to the town instead. It seems I was always in search of the bright lights.

I was born in October 1965, so I'm guessing this would have been a bit before or during 1967's Summer of Love and the whole Flower Power scene, which seems appropriate as most of my early memories have a slightly hazy, psychedelic quality in keeping with the mood of the times.

I remember lying on my back staring at clouds and long afternoons digging for squirrels with my next-door neighbour Rupert (for some reason I thought they lived in underground nests). If it was windy, you might find me running around with my arms out-stretched, hoping a strong gust would carry me into the air. Or else I might just spend the day lounging around the house with no greater concern than making sure I didn't miss *Mary, Mungo and Midge*.

There were still some stresses. As the youngest of five, I was the natural victim of numerous jokes and wind-ups (it's likely why I thought squirrels lived underground), but for the most part I was happy - until the inevitable day when I had to start my education. As Charles Manson, Altamont and a wave of rock star deaths were putting an end to the innocence of the '60s, St John's Primary School was about to have the same effect on mine.

I remember my first day clearly. After introducing herself, our teacher Mrs Watmough said she had a question.

"If it takes four minutes to boil one egg, how long does it take to boil two eggs? Put your hand up if you think the answer is eight minutes."

I was surprised that out of at least 30 kids, I was the only one without their hand up. Mrs W asked how long I thought it would take and then congratulated me for being the only one to get the answer right.

"I was going to say four minutes!" a boy sitting near me said.

Rather than feeling proud, I remember just thinking how stupid everyone else was for thinking it would take twice as long just because you added an extra egg to the water.

A couple of hours later the bell rang for break and I went to my satchel to get the Bazooka Joe bubble gum my mum had given me as a first day treat - to find it gone.

No one had ever stolen anything from me before, and I was genuinely shocked. I told another teacher someone had "pinched" my bubble gum, but instead of trying to find the little crook, she made some "joke" about how you can pinch a person's bottom but not their gum, which even then I thought was lame.

By the time my mum came to collect me, I'd formed a pretty dismal opinion of most of my classmates and teachers. There were some I'd come to like, but for the most part it was a view I saw little reason to significantly revise.

Having now written about all the schools I attended, I can see this was how I felt about all of them. Even at Beacon I seemed to feel constantly at odds with the majority and what we were being taught, to the point that our otherwise super laid-back sociology teacher took me aside after one class and more or less begged me not to keep challenging every point as I was making it impossible for him to teach.

To be fair, this was mainly in relation to feminism, and he was teaching us the then-dominant theory that aside from physical differences, the sexes were essentially the same and the only reason there were fewer women in positions of power or traditionally male occupations like engineering was because of social conditioning and a patriarchal culture that deliberately held them down.

I never doubted the influence of conditioning, but to offer it as the *sole* explanation (as almost every leading feminist maintained) and to ignore biology entirely was plain lunacy to my mind, and yet I was literally laughed at by the whole class for saying there were differences in how male and female brains worked.

That wasn't my only issue. A lot of people think the second wave of feminists were a well-meaning if slightly kooky lot who simply called for things like equal pay and crèche facilities for working mums, but if you check what they said at the time, you'll see it went waaay beyond this, and their reputation as angry man-haters was fully deserved. Even the 'moderate' ones were painting all men as violent would-be rapists, while the real whack jobs like Valerie Solanas actually called for compulsory castration and male gas camps.

When I heard this stuff, I'd think of people like Martin Luther King or Ghandi who gave their lives for peace or just hard-working family types like my dad who adores my mum and worked 55 hours a week to take care of us all. No way was I going to let their nastiness and lies go unchallenged.

To my dismay, these ideas started to filter into the mainstream, until what had been a radical fringe theory became the more or less unchallenged orthodoxy for the political left and even among many to the centre and the right.

Rather than accepting we have different ambitions and interests, any occupation without an equal representation of women was immediately assumed to be the result of discrimination and/or a general failure on society's part to sufficiently encourage women into these areas, leading to various drives and initiatives as well as calls for compulsory quotas (in some countries these were implemented). Serious consideration was given to other feminist proposals, including paying housewives an hourly wage and a particularly scary one for men to be charged with rape if they hadn't received a woman's explicit verbal consent prior to having sex.

The media also got behind the movement. The Guardian gave columns to Suzanne Moore and Germaine Greer (apparently unconcerned at the latter's support for Valerie Solanas), and it was unusual for any supplement not to include at least one feminist-themed article ("Is Your Boss a Secret Sexist?" "How to Turn Your Boyfriend into a New Man," etc.).

The music press also got on the bandwagon. *Melody Maker* began championing 'Riot Grrrl,' a collection of mostly shambolic all-female acts who spent most of their time complaining about how hard it was for women to succeed in the industry (though once you account for the fact there are far fewer women trying to make it, it's clear they are actually massively over-represented) as well as demanding things like female-only labels and radio stations to insulate them from all the sexism. A good 50% of the letters page would also be devoted to some feminist or PC-related issue. I remember a long-running debate on whether some male journalist should have been fired for daring to say he found some female musician 'hot.'

As part of their witch-hunt, MM's Editor called for a boycott of The Rolling Stones until they apologised for the misogyny of 'Under My Thumb', and several other acts including Happy Mondays, The Wonder Stuff and Smashing Pumpkins received almost nothing but negative reviews after refusing to kowtow to the PC agenda.

It was horrible watching politics take precedence over the music, and it was affecting all the arts. You could barely enter a comedy club without having to endure at least one "Aren't men crap?" routine (stereotyping guys was okay apparently as this was "redressing the balance"), and just about every TV show had at least one uber-strong female character who seemed placed purely to challenge preconceptions.

It made for depressing, humourless times. Any mention of innate biological differences risked being dismissed as a chauvinist, making it impossible to have any kind of meaningful debate on the subject.

What frustrated me most is how no one seemed to notice they were arguing two mutually conflicting points, that on the one hand our differences are purely due to social conditioning - and to claim otherwise was evidence of sexism - and on the other, that women were innately more sensitive, nurturing, spiritual, etc. - hence the need for female-only radio stations, etc., and to put them into positions of power.

Not surprisingly, the movement achieved almost nothing that probably wouldn't have happened anyway. Instead they became embroiled in petty in-fighting (witness Greer's un-sisterly attack on

Suzanne Moore for her "fuck-me shoes") and pointless debates on whether wearing make-up was "self-empowering" or conforming to patriarchal ideals of beauty.

I actually think it was ordinary women who paid the highest price as anyone who didn't choose to climb the corporate ladder was basically dismissed as brainwashed and weak. I heard more than one saying they felt guilty just because they quite liked the idea of having kids and not working full time. I also believe this was why chivalry appeared to die out around this time. Men got so fed up of getting abuse just for offering their seat or holding a door open - "You think because I'm a woman I can't open it myself?" as one feminist acquaintance boasted of telling someone - that many stopped bothering.

Another bugbear that arose from this time was digital technology and a general move towards pristine, technically flawless recordings. People were in such a rush to buy the latest digital and transistor gear that valve mics, desks, EQs, etc., now worth thousands, were going for a fraction of that; some was literally junked.

I picked up some amazing gear as a result, so it was great in a way, but it was also a pain because you'd constantly have people telling you to "embrace the new technology" or going on about how a digital piano was actually superior to a real one because it didn't have "imperfections" - or some such bollocks. Whenever we played live, we'd always get the same jokes from the other bands about our "steam-powered" amps or "stone-age" drums. Until we discovered Toe Rag, recording would also be a battle to stop the engineer putting 20 mics on the kit or smothering everything in some tinny-sounding reverb.

Digital also led to the CD. Marketed as a giant leap forward in sound, the first digital mix I heard just sounded cold and lifeless, and I've kept with vinyl to this day.

It's common now for hi-fi buffs to prefer vinyl, and while

recording to digital is still the norm, most engineers will admit it's more because of convenience and cost than preferring the sound. There's been such a turnaround in attitudes that most digital emulations are now sold on their ability to reproduce "analogue warmth," "valve-like distortion," etc. - the very things they were meant to overcome.

Though the backlash had been building for a while, you can almost pinpoint the day the tide officially turned - when the White Stripes' album *Elephant* (also recorded at Toe Rag) went to Number 1. That week The Times ran an article on how they'd used vintage recording equipment and edited the tapes with actual razor blades. Suddenly "old school" methods were back in vogue and Toe Rag (which at this point had been operating for almost 20 years with barely a mention in the music press) suddenly became the coolest studio on the planet.

Feminism/political correctness also died a sudden death (at least in the UK) which I'd say came with the launch of *Loaded* ("the magazine for men who should know better"). It contained unapologetic reviews of lap dancing clubs and articles on how to make your own porn film. After a decade of po-faced political correctness, it seized the Zeitgeist and quickly became one of the UK's biggest selling magazines, followed by a series of imitators including *FHM*, *Nuts* and *Front*.

As 'laddism' became the new buzzword, *Melody Maker* ditched Riot Grrrl, The Guardian gave Greer a gardening column, and it was back to sex, drugs and rock 'n' roll as if Political Correctness had been nothing but a horrible nightmare.

A psychologist reading these various accounts of when I was attacked or ridiculed only to be subsequently vindicated might diagnose some kind of narcissistic disorder or "right man" complex - perhaps the result of the teasing I endured as a child and then reinforced by what happened on my first day at school when I was the only one to correctly answer the question about the eggs.

But as on that occasion, I never thought what I was saying was clever or anything more than common sense, obvious stuff. I wasn't even that original. Outside of a few student and "intellectual" circles, I hardly knew anyone who thought men and women were the same, and the only people who said they preferred a digital piano to a real one were musicians or sound engineers. Ironically, it was the people who were meant to know a thing or two who seemed most likely to get this stuff wrong. So why did so many of them fall for the digital hype, and how come almost no one on the left noticed the contradictions at the heart of feminism?

You won't be surprised I have a theory on this, and it's more or less the same reason I was the only one to get the question right about the eggs, or more importantly, why everyone else got it wrong.

In case you think it's unfair to expect a bunch of 4 to 5-year-olds to get the answer right, I'd point out that their answer was in a way more sophisticated than mine as it required at least a basic understanding of the principles of multiplication (odd in itself given it was our first ever class), and if they knew that much, you'd think at least a few others could have applied the common sense bit - aside from me and the boy who nearly said "four minutes," but for some reason decided against it.

So here's what I think happened.

As I've said, given it was our first class, I find it slightly odd that every one out of 30 or so kids would have understood the basics of multiplication. However, I'd imagine a fair proportion would have. So when Mrs Watmough said, "Put your hand up if you think the answer is eight minutes," a load of these kids shot theirs up, assuming they'd got the answer right. Clever - to an extent - just a bit lacking in common sense.

I'm sure at least some had no knowledge of maths, but rather than admit the fact, and seeing all these kids with their hands in the air and looking confident, decided simply to follow them. You can't blame them for not having been taught any maths yet, and in a way it showed initiative. They just backed the wrong horse in this case.

Which just leaves myself (who merely applied common sense) and the boy who nearly said "four minutes," but then changed his mind. He could have been lying, but I reckon he was telling the truth and that he wasn't the only one to suspect the right answer. However, by this point the majority of the class now had their hands up, and so they began to doubt themselves. "Can I really be right and all these others wrong? And if I am wrong, how will they react? Do I really want to risk being laughed at by the whole class?" So they decided to play safe and went with the majority.

I have a confession. After recounting this story, I started having my own doubts. Would a teacher really ask such a question to a class of 4 to 5-year-olds on their first day? I'm certain it happened at some point as I can picture it clearly. I even remember who nearly said "four minutes" (Garry, who I later shared the Old Kent Road squat with). Also, my memory of the pram incident proved accurate, and that was even earlier. Still, it is possible this occurred at some later date (the first day of another term possibly?) and I subconciously moved it to my first day to make myself and the story more interesting - which I realise won't help my assertion that I'm not suffering from some kind of personality disorder. I doubt it would have been much later as more people would have been familiar with the concept of the "trick question" and understood basic maths, but whenever it was, the question was the right level of difficulty to have produced the wrong answer from almost everyone in the class, and that's what is important here - trust me.

Okay, so now let's apply what happened then to how a flawed theory can become accepted by a majority of apparently intelligent people using as my example the feminists' assertion that the sexes are essentially the same and the only reason there are fewer female bosses or engineers is because of social conditioning and/or sexism.

For a theory to become accepted, it can't sound too insane and there needs to be at least some supporting evidence. Thus Greer, et al., talked of how children are given different toys to play with - dolls for girls, guns for boys, etc. - demonstrating how early the conditioning starts as well as differing expectations and standards applied throughout life.

All pretty reasonable so far. Though, of course, it assumes this differing treatment is the cause or *sole* cause of our differing behaviour rather than a response to it. A bit of common sense or real-world observation (e.g., watching kids in a playground) would quickly reveal how deep the differences run. Unfortunately, the sort of people who are drawn to fashionable new theories tend by definition to be a bit lacking in the common sense/real world experience department. (This is also why "experts" are often more prone to believing a flawed theory than the general public.)

We might compare these early adopters to the first group of kids who put their hand up when Mrs Watmough asked who thought it would take eight minutes to boil two eggs.

Others may also be drawn to the theory for personal reasons (e.g., women who've had particularly negative experiences with men) or some vested interest (e.g., writers hoping to carve out a media career. Or in the case of CDs and digital, equipment manufacturers and labels trying to resell their back catalogues).

If enough people start supporting the new theory, it starts gaining momentum, allowing them to force the issue - "So why do *you* think there are fewer women in power or mechanics? Are you suggesting we're not capable? Maybe you think we should all just stay in the kitchen?"

A lot of people won't have even considered the question until now, or they just aren't that interested, but they must now state their position. Rather than admit they don't know or have to give some alternative explanation, many just go for the easy option and agree with the new theory: "No, you're absolutely right. It's because they're being held back by men. They probably feel threatened."

We can compare these people to the second group of kids who went along with the first lot. Not stupid necessarily, just uninformed or not that interested.

Not everyone will be convinced by the new theory, but with so many people now supporting it, they may start to doubt themselves ("Can I be right and all these others wrong?") or they keep their doubts to themselves to avoid attack or being ridiculed – just like the kid/s who nearly said "four minutes," but decided against it.

Which just leaves a minority of opinionated, argumentative types like myself to battle it out with everyone.

The longer a theory has been around, the older and less fashionable it becomes, while cracks start to reveal themselves. This leaves the ground fertile for a fresh challenge or for an older theory to return - perhaps modified slightly to counter its original flaws.

This can happen gradually over a long period, but often something comes along that seems so fresh and exciting in comparison, it renders the now-old theory almost instantly out of date, as when *Loaded* magazine first appeared or when the White Stripes went to Number 1 with *Elephant*.

Now everything goes into reverse as the old theory becomes a rapidly sinking ship with everyone jumping off, lest they find themselves clinging on alone.

Those who suspected it was flawed can now admit to their doubts ("I never really believed men and women were the same"/"I was going to say four minutes.") The ones who didn't know or didn't care move to the new theory, leaving the original proponents to either admit they got it wrong or get used to being the ones having to constantly defend their position.

Strangely, it's the most vocal proponents of a theory who are often the quickest to jump ship, even if it's to one they once derided - as when certain music paper editors reinvented themselves as beer-guzzling rock 'n' rollers the moment the PC ship went down. However, one should not be surprised by this, nor expect any acknowledgement of their shameless U-turn as they never really gave a shit about the theory in the first place, only what they could get out of it personally - be it to further their own careers or simply as an opportunity to point their fingers and feel superior. The henchmen of every movement - too stupid to come up with their own ideas and too cowardly to stand for the truth - these are the people one needs to be most wary of.

No doubt many will find my attempts to extrapolate the behaviour of a class of children on their first day at school to the rise of feminism and digital technology as both unfair and simplistic. But I maintain it is valid, as we are talking about the fundamentals of human nature - the need to belong, fear of ridicule, etc., which exist regardless of age or intellect. In fact, the pressure to conform is often stronger among adults, especially if one's livelihood depends on it. If Joe Bloggs says men and women are innately different, he might get into the occasional argument, but if a college professor says it, he could find himself professionally ostracised and unable to work (as has happened in the US). This is another reason "experts" can be more likely to get these things wrong than the general public.

And I would go further and say it's because of these patterns that numerous flawed theories and ideologies became widely accepted throughout history. So often we look back and ask how entire nations, including many intellectuals of the time, could have fallen for some easily disproven theory or backed some ideology espoused by some clearly deranged leader, resulting in wars, persecutions and tyranny - as if gripped by some collective mass insanity. Five minutes of calm, rational thinking can reveal the unworkability of both communism and unfettered capitalism, and untold human misery could have been avoided.

Some of the biggest atrocities have been committed in the name of religion. The Catholic Church has a particularly dark history due in part to the notion of Papal Infallibility and the idea that any edict should be treated as coming directly from God.

Yet we know this can't be true from the simple fact that previous edicts have been reversed, as when Pope Pius VII finally accepted that the planets revolved around the Sun and not the Earth. This also went against the Book of Genesis, destroying the other central tenet of Catholicism, that the Bible is also God's word and cannot be questioned. There are other examples of contradictary teachings, but one is enough to demonstrate the point. That's not to say all of it is untrue or that it doesn't contain important wisdom, just that it can and should be challenged.

If religion seems an easy target, science has also been guilty of such behaviour. In the 1980s the British Medical Association declared the entirety of alternative medicine, including Chinese medicine and all ancient and herbal remedies, as ineffective. Any apparent successes or cures in their view would either have happened anyway or were the result of the "placebo effect" (the patient's own belief that the treatment would work).

Within five years they'd completely reversed their position, leading to acupuncture and even spiritual healing becoming available on the NHS – with no major outcry from its members.

This was a massive turnaround, given many of these therapies are based on unproven concepts such as "chi" (a unifying life force) or the "meridian system" (a map of invisible energy points around the body) which go against the fundamental principles of orthodox medicine. You'd therefore expect some compelling new research or studies to have forced it, yet there was none, or none they cited. What had happened during this time was an explosion of the public's interest in alternative therapies, with support from the media and some famous figures including Prince Charles. An old theory had returned to fashion.

Instead of the respected pillars of the community that doctors were used to being treated as, those who continued to dismiss such therapies as "old wives' tales" or "snake oil" were now looking very out of touch. So at the first opportunity, they jumped ship - "to hell with the scientific method; we want to be liked again."

These patterns can also be observed among supposedly anti-establishment groups. Witness the rapid death of both the Yippie movement in the '70s and the Militant Socialists of the '80s and how their leaders were the first to sell out, moving into careers like PR and finance (step forward Derek Hatton).

And it's happening now. Crazy political decisions with easily foreseeable, disastrous consequences are being made constantly. Just recently the UK Foreign Secretary Jack Straw tried to make it a criminal offence to "insult a religion." Five minutes of level-headed thinking would show the impossibility of enforcing such a law. How does one define a religion? Or an insult? Might I be arrested for making a bishop and actress joke? Or for saying I think public stonings are barbaric? Not to mention the wider implications for free speech.

The proposal was defeated, but only by a narrow margin. Nearly half of what are meant to be our finest political minds thought this ill-thought-out piece of lunacy was a good idea.

The law was an attempt to ease tensions in the wake of the Iraq invasion and so-called "War on Terror." Again, a few minutes of rational thought would have revealed the lies told in the run-up as well as the insanity of waging war against a faceless enemy with no geographical base. The consequences were both predictable and predicted – yet it was supported by almost every politician from all sides in both the UK and the US. And now we're caught in an unwinnable war that could last for decades if it doesn't lead to World War 3.

I tried to avoid the phrase, but what I've really been talking about is "herd mentality." My reluctance is because it implies the people are stupid, when in most cases it's more to do with them not having the time to research these subjects. This is especially true of politics, at least as far as the general public are concerned, due to the complexity of some of the issues involved as well as the fact that most simply find the subject incredibly boring.

Even if one can be bothered to learn about the history and arguments that led to the Balfour Declaration (as just one example), how much difference will it even make? You still end up with one vote every four to five years just like everyone else and a selection of candidates you might not even agree with.

So you can't really blame people for deciding to leave the complex, boring stuff to others and focussing on personal issues that they can have a direct influence on. Unfortunately, this makes it very easy for politicians to take advantage. All they have to do is make some voter-friendly promises to lower taxes and tackle crime, and as long as they seem sincere, few will look much further. By the time they realise they've actually voted in some warmongering psychopath, the damage will have been done. In extreme cases they may use violence or start enacting laws to ensure they can never be removed.

As these patterns seem rooted in human nature, are we therefore destined to repeat them forever - locked in an endless cycle of war and destruction, only waking up when it's too late, until we finally annihilate ourselves once and for all?

Possibly, but not necessarily. The reason I have some optimism is that I don't actually accept those people who supported tyrants were as unaware of their potential for evil as they may claim and that there is usually a point before they gained power and could still have been stopped when it should have been obvious what they were about even to someone with little interest in politics.

Take George W Bush. When first campaigning for President, it was widely reported that while Governor of Texas, he rejected every single plea for clemency from prisoners awaiting execution (the only Governor to do so), rarely spending more than a few minutes deliberating a case and often going to dinner straight after.

So can one really claim surprise that he would later have such an appalling human rights record or be so gung-ho about going to war? Even if one missed that story, by the time he stood for re-election, many of those war crimes, human rights abuses, etc., had been revealed, yet he still won a second term. Many even applauded him for his 'tough' stance.

I'm not suggesting every person who voted for him was evil. Had it been their fellow Americans being indiscriminately bombed and tortured, I think most would have been appalled. But because it was happening to people who spoke a different language or worshipped a different God, they could dismiss them as 'lesser' and not deserving of the same rights.

But if you view every human as a kind of distant relative (which in reality they are), it becomes almost impossible to accept such stuff. You don't have to share their views, and as with an immediate family member, they might even drive you mad, but you still wouldn't wish active harm on them and would only turn to violence if directly threatened or as an absolute last resort (which was not the case in Iraq, despite Bush's claims) - and even then you'd keep it to the barest minimum.

This isn't as big a leap as it sounds. As I've said, most already apply this attitude to their own countrymen, who, after all, don't all think alike or even share the same religion - we just need to extend it a bit further. Not everyone has to do this either. A swing of just 1% would have kept Bush out of office.

The first blatant human rights violation and we should withdraw our support forever. This would prevent potential psychopaths from ever gaining a foothold as well as creating a vacuum for more honest candidates to come through.

Had we applied these principles, we'd never have gone to war on such flimsy evidence and would have probably avoided the problem in the first place by withdrawing support when Bush Sr continued selling arms to Saddam Hussein after he'd gassed the Kurds.

It's too easy to blame people like Bush and Blair for all our problems. We have to accept our own responsibility for voting for them in the first place or continuing to support them once it was clear what sort of people they were. This might mean voting against one's personal interests, but at some point you have to ask whether some minor tax advantage or whatever is more important than the suffering of millions.

If we want, we can take it further by refusing to support corporations that act unethically. With targeted worldwide boycotts, even a multinational can be brought to its knees in a relatively short time, and with the internet, it's never been easier to mobilise support. There's a lot more of us than them. We just need to harness our power.

The real question is not whether we can change the world, rather are we prepared to slightly inconvenience ourselves in order to achieve it. But if we continue putting a small personal interest above bombing whole countries and buying into this simplistic "You're either for us or against us" and "good guys/bad guys" crap, then this shit will continue, and it will eventually bite us in the ass.

I know it's not easy to be constantly high-minded, and

sometimes you have no choice but to vote for the lesser of two evils, but we can at least try - try to be honest, try to be decent, try not to hurt others.

It wasn't my intention for this to turn into a political sermon, but at some point it started going its own way, and I decided to go with it. We're facing so many political and environmental disasters right now, and we haven't got time to fuck around. It's time to make peace fashionable again, but this time without the naïvety. And who knows - if enough people get on board, maybe others will jump ship and follow.

After writing the above, I started wondering what my real point was and realised it's that love really is the answer. It's not just a possible solution; it's the only solution.

(This essay was expanded on after its initial writing, see also 'End Notes.')

END NOTES

Thurs 26 Oct 2006

So that's it, I've written my 30 essays, and I now have my book. It's been a very interesting experience, and apart from my one dark night of the soul (see 'Ames, Aims, and Amie'), I've enjoyed it. I'm pretty knackered, though, and I'm looking forward to a break and getting back to making some music.

As a final update, Toby moved out yesterday. He turned out to be a good house-mate. We had some good chats, and he didn't rip my stuff off. Whatever Amie was upset about seems to have resolved itself, and she's been in much better spirits. I should also thank her for lending me *I Love You More Than You Know* which inspired this and to Jonathan Ames for writing it, and I'd also like to thank you, Dear Reader, for getting this far and putting up with all my rants and self-indulgence.

POSTSCRIPT

I knew when I finished these essays there'd be some editing to do. I didn't realise how much, though, until I came back to them. Some of the longer ones were in particularly bad shape with sketched-out sections and pages of notes. Mostly it was the same cutting, moving and fine-tuning I've referred to a few times, which I'd have done at the time had I not set myself such a tight schedule, but there's probably another 10-15% of additional ideas that weren't in the original draft which I thought I should mention in the interests of full disclosure. I hope that hasn't ruined it for you.

Tim Briffa.

Printed in Great Britain
by Amazon